S0-ADY-159

Study Guide and Workbook

for

Haviland, Prins, Walrath, and McBride's

Cultural Anthropology
The Human Challenge

Eleventh Edition

M. L. Miranda
University of Nevada, Las Vegas

THOMSON
✳
™
WADSWORTH

Australia • Canada • Mexico • Singapore • Spain • United Kingdom • United States

COPYRIGHT © 2005 Wadsworth, a division of
Thomson Learning, Inc. Thomson Learning™ is a
trademark used herein under license.

ALL RIGHTS RESERVED. No part of this work
covered by the copyright hereon may be reproduced
or used in any form or by any means—graphic,
electronic, or mechanical, including but not limited to
photocopying, recording, taping, Web distribution,
information networks, or information storage and
retrieval systems—without the written permission of
the publisher.

Printed in the United States of America
1   2   3   4   5   6   7   08   07   06   05   04

Printer: Globus Printing

0-534-62490-1

For more information about our products,
contact us at:
Thomson Learning Academic Resource Center
1-800-423-0563

For permission to use material from this text or
product, submit a request online at
http://www.thomsonrights.com.
Any additional questions about permissions can be
submitted by email to **thomsonrights@thomson.com.**

Thomson Wadsworth
10 Davis Drive
Belmont, CA 94002-3098
USA

Asia
Thomson Learning
5 Shenton Way #01-01
UIC Building
Singapore 068808

Australia/New Zealand
Thomson Learning
102 Dodds Street
Southbank, Victoria 3006
Australia

Canada
Nelson
1120 Birchmount Road
Toronto, Ontario M1K 5G4
Canada

Europe/Middle East/South Africa
Thomson Learning
High Holborn House
50/51 Bedford Row
London WC1R 4LR
United Kingdom

Latin America
Thomson Learning
Seneca, 53
Colonia Polanco
11560 Mexico D.F.
Mexico

Spain/Portugal
Paraninfo
Calle/Magallanes, 25
28015 Madrid, Spain

Introduction:
Why Should You Use the *Study Guide* and *Workbook*?

Your instructor may or may not require the use of this study guide and workbook to accompany William Haviland's textbook, *Cultural Anthropology: The Human Challenge, Eleventh Edition.* However, there are some important reasons why you might find it helpful as you begin your study of anthropology.

First of all, using a study guide and workbook along with the main textbook for the course forces you to simply spend time with the material. You have probably found that when you think you have read an assignment for a course, often you actually can't recall much of what you read. By adding time to your reading for answering review questions, going over key vocabulary, and so on, you fix the information in your memory in a far more thorough manner. The time you spend each day on your study guide and workbook will help you to spend less time "cramming" for exams later on.

Secondly, putting things in your own words, as the study guide and workbook requires, is the best way to make the subject your own. Education researchers agree that this is a good way to ensure that simple memorization is replaced by true comprehension of information. In addition, the exercises which encourage you to grasp concepts rather than memorize words will help you on tests, where your instructor may phrase things in different ways than your textbook author does. This workbook also offers you the opportunity to construct charts which will help you in studying, to do exercises based on maps and diagrams that can visually fix the material in your mind, and to apply anthropological methods to various real life problems. Make the book your own; write in it; do the exercises you find useful and skip the ones you don't. This guide was prepared to help you.

Each chapter of the Study Guide and Workbook contains several sections. A *synopsis* of the chapter is followed by an outline of *what you should learn from the chapter.* Then comes a section of *key terms and names* for you to define or identify and a list of *review questions* which can be answered in a few sentences. There is also a *fill-in-the-blank* section to help you review. In addition to *exercises* which range from the very difficult to the playful, there are *multiple- choice practice questions, true/false practice questions, practice matching sets, short answer questions,* and *practice essays.* These are excellent ways of preparing for the various kinds of examinations your instructor may prepare. Your instructor may also choose to use parts of this study guide for homework or extra credit assignments.

If used conscientiously this book will be a helpful complement to your textbook.

M.L. Miranda
University of Nevada, Las Vegas

Table of Contents

Chapter 1

The Essence of Anthropology

Synopsis

This chapter introduces the discipline of anthropology, the study of humankind everywhere, throughout time. Anthropology seeks to produce useful generalizations about people and their behavior, to arrive at the fullest possible understanding of human diversity, and to understand those things that all human beings have in common. There are two major subfields of anthropology: physical anthropology and cultural anthropology. Physical anthropology focuses on the biological aspects of being human while cultural anthropology focuses on human beings as members of society. Because of anthropology's holistic perspective, it can contribute substantially to the resolution of human problems.

What You Should Learn from This Chapter

I.   Learn how anthropology helps us to better understand ourselves:
- A.   explore the impulse to find out who we are and where we came from
- B.   explain how and why the discipline emerged and developed
- C.   describe anthropology's relationship to the other social sciences

II.   Know the subfields of anthropology and understand their purpose and practice:
- A.   physical anthropology
- B.   archaeology
- C.   linguistics
- D.   ethnology

III. Appreciate how anthropologists conduct their research and the limits on such research.

IV.   Understand anthropology's relationship to the "hard sciences" and to the humanities:
- A.   the hypothesis-testing framework

V.   Think about some of the ethical issues that confront anthropologists today.

Key Terms

Anthropology
Archaeology
Comparative Approach
Cultural Anthropology
Cultural Deprivation
Culture-bound
Ethnography
Ethnology
Forensic Anthropology

Globalization
Holistic Perspective
Hypothesis
Linguistic Anthropology
Molecular Anthropology
Participant Observation
Physical Anthropology
Theory

Exercise

Review Questions

1. What are the four subfields of anthropology? How are they related to each other?

2. In their research, how do anthropologists attempt to be as objective and free from cultural bias as possible?

3. Distinguish between ethnology and ethnography.

4. Explain in what sense anthropology is a relatively recent product of Western civilization.

5. How does anthropology use the research of many other disciplines?

6. Why are anthropology and sociology closely allied? What sets them apart?

7. Cultural adaptation, development, and evolution are three general concerns of anthropologists. How are they interrelated?

8. Why do archaeologists excavate sites from the historical period when many documents provide information on recent culture?

9. What is the significance of "The Garbage Project?"

10. Why did archaeologists have difficulty in interpreting remains of large Mayan settlements in Central America?

11. With what aspects of language are linguists concerned?

12. Discuss why anthropology is considered the "most liberating of all sciences."

13. Distinguish between the social sciences and the humanities.

14. Discuss how human behavior and biology are inextricably intertwined. Provide examples.

15. Explain why it took so long for a systematic discipline of anthropology to appear.

16. Explain how the work of an anthropological linguist can contribute to our understanding of the human past.

17. Discuss the problems inherent in scientific anthropology.

18. Discuss the ethical problems that could arise in the process of anthropological research.

19. How do linguists aid in our study of the past?

20. Describe the role of the ethnologist, giving an example of the sort of study an ethnologist would produce.

21. What is participant-observation? What are its advantages and disadvantages when compared to other social science methods?

22. Why might it be advisable to do research outside one's own culture prior to studying one's own?

23. What is meant by cross-cultural comparison? What significance does it have?

24. How did anthropologist Philleo Nash affect the policies of the Roosevelt and Truman administrations?

25. What are the two key elements in the derivation of scientific laws, according to Haviland?

26. Explain the "self-correcting" nature of science, and give an example.

27. What are the limitations of the scientific approach, according to Haviland?

28. What problems are encountered when using the questionnaire for information gathering in ethnographic research?

29. How were anthropologists able to aid in the understanding of exchange relations in rural Peru?

30. What might be accomplished by research into one particular culture?

31. What distinguishes anthropology from the "hard sciences?"

32. Why must anthropologists exercise caution prior to publishing the results of their research?

33. To whom are anthropologists ultimately responsible?

34. How did Laura Nader explain her ethical position with regard to her work on the Zapotec and on U.S. energy research?

35. What is meant by a "global community?"

Fill-in-the-Blank

1. Anthropology is the study of _____ everywhere, throughout time.

2. Anthropology is one of several disciplines in the social and natural sciences that study humans. It differs from other disciplines primarily in its ability to _____ data from many sources.

3. Anthropologists recognize that human behavior has both _____ and social/cultural aspects.

4. Anthropology is divided into four branches, one of _____ anthropology and three of _____ anthropology (archaeology, linguistics, and ethnology).

5. An example of a practical application of physical anthropology is _____ anthropology, in which anthropologists testify in legal situations concerning human skeletal remains.

6. Archaeology is the study of culture based on _____ remains.

7. An in-depth description of a specific culture is called an _____ .

8. Comparisons of "housework" shows that _____ spend less time on household tasks than Westerners do with all their time-saving gadgets.

9. A tentative explanation of the relation between certain phenomena (e.g., "The light failed to work because the filament was broken") is called a _____ .

10. When archaeologists studied the Classic period of Maya civilization, they assumed that tropical forests occupied by people practicing _____ could not support large population clusters.

11. Anthropological research is just as likely to be funded by the National Science Foundation as it is by the National Endowment for the _____ .

12. Whatever distinctions people may claim for themselves, they are _____ specifically, _____ , and as such, they share a common ancestry with others like apes and monkeys.

13. The physical anthropologist applies all the techniques of modern _____ to achieve fuller understanding of human variation and the ways in which it relates to the different environments in which people lived.

14. Today, _____ , or the anthropological study of genes and genetic relationships, is another vital component of biological anthropology.

15. The term _____ refers to worldwide interconnectedness, signified by global movements of natural resources, trade goods, human labor, finance capital, information, and infectious diseases.

16. A _____ , or dogma, is an assertion of opinion or belief formally handed down by authority as true and indisputable.

Multiple-Choice Practice Questions

1. Anthropology is _____.
   a. the study of Western culture primarily through the analysis of its folklore
   b. the study of humankind everywhere, throughout time
   c. the study of nonhuman primates through behavioral analysis
   d. the study of the species Homo sapiens by analyzing its biological but not its cultural dimensions
   e. the analysis of humankind from the subjective perspective of one group

2. The systematic study of humans as biological organisms.
   a. linguistic anthropology
   b. cultural ecology
   c. cultural anthropology
   d. archaeology
   e. None of these

3. Anthropology differs from other disciplines that study humans in its ability to _____ data from many sources.
   a. synthesize
   b. eliminate
   c. invent
   d. falsify
   e. fabricate

4. Anthropology is traditionally divided into four branches, one of _____ anthropology and three of _____ anthropology.

   a. cultural/physical

   b. physical/cultural

   c. archaeological/linguistic

   d. ethnological/physical

   e. biological/physical

5. As part of your job, you may study the frequency of blood types in human populations, watch the behavior of monkeys and apes, or dig for early hominid bones from East Africa. You are a/an _____.

   a. entymologist

   b. primatologist

   c. ethnologist

   d. physical anthropologist

   e. cultural anthropologist

6. Theories about the world and reality based on the assumptions and values of one's own culture are_____.

   a. simplistic

   b. irrational

   c. culture-bound.

   d. relativistic

   e. inductive

7. An archaeologist might attempt to _____.

   a. study material remains to reconstruct past cultures

   b. study present languages to reconstruct when they diverged from a parent stock

   c. study garbage to explain contemporary behavior

   d. "study material remains to reconstruct past cultures", "study present languages to reconstruct when they diverged from a parent stock" and "study garbage to explain contemporary behavior"

   e. "study material remains to reconstruct past cultures" and "study garbage to explain contemporary behavior"

8. An archaeologist studies_____.

   a. potsherds

   b. paleoecology

   c. genetic drift

   d. garbage

   e. potsherds, paleoecology and garbage

9. _____ is that branch of anthropology concerned with humans as biological organisms.

    a. Archaeology

    b. Cultural anthropology

    c. Ethnology

    d. Physical anthropology

    e. Paleontology

10. The focus of anthropology is on both evolution and culture as such it is able _____

    a. to address the "nature versus nurture" question

    b. to address certain ethical issues

    c. to discuss the efficacy of various research methods

    d. to address the qualitative vs. quantitative methods issue

    e. to address the political questions of the day

11. In-depth descriptive studies of specific cultures are called _____

    a. ethnologies

    b. ethnobotanies

    c. biologies

    d. ethnographies

    e. anthropologies

12. The study of two or more cultures is called a/an _____

    a. ethnology

    b. case study.

    c. ethnography

    d. biography

    e. ethnohistory

13. Anthropologists doing fieldwork typically involve themselves in many different experiences. They try to investigate not just one aspect of culture (such as the political system) but how all aspects relate to each other (for example, how the political system fits with economic institutions, religious beliefs, etc.). This approach is called the _____ perspective.

    a. holistic

    b. ethnological

    c. sociocultural

    d. sociological

    e. culture-bound

14. Ethnographic fieldwork _____.
    a. is usually associated with the study of wealthy elites.
    b. is usually associated with the study of North American society.
    c. is usually associated with the study of non-Western peoples.
    d. can be applied, with useful results, to the study of North American peoples.
    e. "is usually associated with the study of non-Western peoples" and "can be applied, with useful results, to the study of North American peoples"

15. Ethnographic research on the cultural deprivation theories of the 1960s helped to demonstrate that _____.
    a. minority children are culturally deprived
    b. cultural deprivation causes lack of achievement in minority children
    c. the theory that minority children fail to achieve because they are culturally deprived is true
    d. the theory that minority children fail to achieve because they are culturally deprived is a culture-bound theory
    e. "minority children are culturally deprived", "cultural deprivation causes lack of achievement in minority children" and "the theory that minority children fail to achieve because they are culturally deprived is true"

16. Besides being interested in descriptions of particular cultures, the ethnologist is interested in _____.
    a. teaching food foragers how to use time saving gadgets
    b. cross-cultural comparisons
    c. descriptions of nonhuman species
    d. promoting Western ways
    e. providing data to various government agencies to help them suppress certain groups

17. The goal of science is _____.
    a. to discover the universal principles that govern the workings of the visible world
    b. to develop explanations of the world that are testable and correctable
    c. to eliminate the need to use the imagination
    d. "to discover the universal principles that govern the workings of the visible world", "to develop explanations of the world that are testable and correctable" and "to eliminate the need to use the imagination"
    e. "to discover the universal principles that govern the workings of the visible world" and "to develop explanations of the world that are testable and correctable"

18. Archaeologists studying the Classic period Mayan civilization before about 1960 made culture-bound assumptions that the Classic Maya _____.
    a. were more developed than present populations in their forms of agriculture
    b. were food foragers
    c. practiced the same slash-and-burn cultivation that people do today, and therefore could not have lived in large, permanent settlements
    d. lived in large, permanent settlements based on slash-and-burn cultivation
    e. were industrialists with space-age technology

19. Questionnaire surveys _____.
    a. enable anthropologists to discover unexpected patterns of behavior
    b. are never used by anthropologists
    c. are used by anthropologists to supplement information gained by some other means
    d. are used only by sociologists
    e. get at real (versus ideal) patterns of behavior

20. Ideally, on which of the following are theories in cultural anthropology based?
    a. intensive fieldwork done in a single society
    b. ethnographies from all over the world so that statements made about culture will be universally applicable
    c. worldwide questionnaire surveys
    d. intuitive thinking about society and culture based on experiences in one's own society
    e. the theories about culture formulated by the people one has studied

21. Anthropology studies the language of a culture, its philosophy, and its forms of art. In the process of doing research, ethnographers involve themselves intensively in the lives of those they study, trying to experience culture from their informants' points of view. In this sense, anthropology is _____.
    a. scientific
    b. humanistic
    c. radical
    d. conservative
    e. systematic

22. In the writing and dissemination of research material the anthropologist has to consider obligations to various entities. Which of the following would *not* be one of the groups the anthropologist would be obligated to?
    a. the profession of anthropology
    b. the people who funded the study
    c. the people studied
    d. the anthropologist's parents
    e. None of these

23. Linguistic anthropology is concerned with _____.

    a. the description of language

    b. the history of language

    c. how language reflects a people's understanding of the world around them

    d. "the description of language" and "the history of language"

    e. "the description of language", "the history of language" and "how language reflects a people's understanding of the world around them"

24. Throughout most of their history people relied on _____ and _____ for answers to questions about who they are, where they came from, and why they act as they do.

    a. myth

    b. careful observation

    c. systematic testing of data

    d. folklore

    e. myth and folklore

25. By scientifically approaching how people live, anthropologists have learned a great deal about both human _____ and _____

    a. frailties and strengths

    b. instincts and behavior

    c. differences and similarities

    d. insensitivity and callousness

    e. sensitivity and warmth

26. It was not until the late _____ century that a significant number of Europeans considered the behavior of others different from them to be at all relevant to an understanding of themselves.

    a. nineteenth

    b. twentieth

    c. seventeenth

    d. fourteenth

    e. eighteenth

27. As _____ of data anthropologists are well-prepared to understand the findings of other disciplines.

    a. organizers

    b. synthesizers

    c. analyzers

    d. legitimizers

    e. gatherers

28. Another name for physical anthropology is _____.

    a. primatology

    b. evolutionary biology

    c. bio-ecology

    d. biological anthropology

    e. forensic anthropology

29. Although humans are all members of a single species, we differ from each other in some obvious and not so obvious ways. Which of the following would be ways that human differ?

    a. skin color

    b. the shape of various physical features

    c. biochemical factors

    d. susceptibility to certain diseases

    e. "skin color", "the shape of various physical features", "biochemical factors" and "susceptibility to certain diseases"

30. According to Haviland, we may think of culture as the often unconscious standards by which groups of people operate. These standards are _____.

    a. genetically transmitted

    b. biologically inherited

    c. learned

    d. absorbed by osmosis

    e. None of these

31. Another name for sociocultural anthropology is _____.

    a. ethnology

    b. ethnography

    c. cultural ecology

    d. ethnology, ethnography and cultural ecology

    e. None of these

32. The archaeologist is able to find out about human behavior in the past, far beyond the mere _____ years to which historians are limited, by their dependence upon written records.

    a. 20,000

    b. 10,000

    c. 5,000

    d. 7,000

    e. 8,000

33. Anthropological research techniques are applicable for which of the following research subjects?
    a. the study of non-western peoples
    b. the study of health care delivery systems
    c. schools
    d. corporate bureaucracies
    e. "the study of non-western peoples", "the study of health care delivery systems", "schools" and "corporate bureaucracies"

34. _____ is/are another hallmark of anthropology.
    a. Case studies
    b. Surveys
    c. Random sampling
    d. Cross-cultural comparisons
    e. None of these

35. In a sense, one may think of _____ as the study of alternative ways of doing things.
    a. participant observation
    b. ethnography
    c. ethnology
    d. case studies
    e. None of these

36. One well known forensic anthropologist is _____.
    a. Sheilagh Brooks
    b. Bernardo Arriaza
    c. Jennifer Thompson
    d. Clyde C. Snow
    e. None of these

37. From skeletal remains, the forensic anthropologist can **not** establish which of following?
    a. stature
    b. race
    c. sex
    d. marital status
    e. age

38. A pioneering American anthropologist, who did work among the Zuni and founded the Women's Anthropological Society in 1885.
    a. Margaret Mead
    b. Ruth Benedict
    c. Martha Knack
    d. Margaret Lyneis
    e. Matilda Coxe Stevenson

39. Through the efforts of _____ many of the great anthropology museums were established.

    a. Franz Boas

    b. Bronislaw Malinowski

    c. John Wesley Powell

    d. Leslie White

    e. Fredric Ward Putnam

40. He established the Bureau of American Ethnology in 1879.

    a. Robert Kroeber

    b. George Peter Murdock

    c. John Wesley Powell

    d. Sean Conlin

    e. Clyde Wood

41. Which of the following services is **not** one that forensic anthropologists are routinely called upon by the police and other authorities to do?

    a. identify potential archaeological sites

    b. identify the remains of murder victims

    c. identify missing persons

    d. identify people who have died in disasters

    e. identify victims of genocide

42. Among the skeletal remains studied by forensic anthropologist Clyde Snow are the remains of _____.

    a. Julius Caesar

    b. General George A. Custer

    c. Adolf Hitler

    d. Josef Mengele

    e. General George A. Custer and Josef Mengele

43. This woman anthropologist was hired by the Bureau of American Ethnology in 1888, making her one of the first women in the U.S. to receive a full-time position in science.

    a. Margaret Mead

    b. Ruth Benedict

    c. Matilda Coxe Stevenson

    d. Laura Nader

    e. Martha Knack

44. _____ and his students made anthropology courses a common part of college and university curricula.

    a. John Wesley Powell

    b. Fredric Ward Putnam

    c. Bronislaw Malinowski

    d. Claude Levi-Strauss

    e. Franz Boas

45. His classification of Indian languages north of Mexico is still consulted by scholars today.

    a. Franz Boas

    b. Noam Chomsky

    c. Gary Palmer

    d. John Wesley Powell

    e. George Urioste

46. Although the sciences and humanities are often thought of as mutually exclusive approaches they do share some common methods for certain activities. Which of the following activities is *not* common to both the humanities and sciences?

    a. critical thinking

    b. mental creativity

    c. innovation

    d. data gathering

    e. None of these

47. Haviland, the author of your textbook, has identified two countries that have made moves toward allowing same sex unions. Identify the two countries.

    a. Mexico and Sweden

    b. Brazil and the Netherlands

    c. Afghanistan and Pakistan

    d. Italy and Greece

    e. The United States and Canada

48. The terrorist attacks on the World Trade Center and the Pentagon would be of interest to which sub-discipline of anthropology?

    a. archaeology

    b. economic anthropology

    c. ethnology

    d. forensic anthropology

    e. medical anthropology

49. As shown in your textbook, forensic anthropologist _____ works at piecing together the remains of victims of state-sponsored terrorism in Bosnia.

    a. Eva Nowak

    b. Clyde Woods

    c. Jennifer Thompson

    d. John Wesley Powell

    e. Mamphela Ramphele

50. _____based on knowledge are essential in every culture, and culture is our species' ticket to survival.

    a. Assimilation

    b. Acculturation

    c. Adaptations

    d. Simulations

    e. Dispensations

51. Made possible by means of sophisticated communications, human cultures developed the physical capacity for which of the following?

    a. tool use

    b. mental telepathy

    c. complex language

    d. accumulating wealth

    e. A and C

52. Anthropologists do their work within _____subfields of the discipline.

    a. one

    b. two

    c. ten

    d. seven

    e. four

53. In anthropology, tentative explanations of observed phenomena concerning humankind are known as _____.

    a. theories

    b. hypotheses

    c. opinions

    d. patterns

    e. facsimiles

54. As experts in the anatomy of human bones and tissues, _____lend their knowledge about the body to applied areas such as gross anatomy laboratories and to criminal investigations.

    a. ethnographers

    b. linguistic anthropologists

    c. ethnologists

    d. physical anthropologists

    e. archaeologists

55. The study of living and fossil primates falls with the purview of_____.

    a. primatology

    b. osteology.

    c. paleopathology.

    d. forensic anthropology.

    e. archaeology.

56. Which of the following areas would not be of interest to the physical anthropologist?

    a. genes and genetic relationships.

    b. growth and development.

    c. human evolution.

    d. political behavior.

    e. human adaptation.

57. If I were called by the local police department's crime scene investigation unit to identify a murder victim, I would probably be a _____.

    a. medical anthropologists.

    b. forensic anthropologists.

    c. paleoanthropologist.

    d. paleoarchaeologist.

    e. forensic entymologist.

58. Using anthropological knowledge and methods to solve practical problems falls within the realm of _____.

    a. ethnology.

    b. ethnography.

    c. medical anthropology.

    d. forensic anthropology.

    e. applied anthropology.

59. Explanations for natural or cultural phenomena, supported by a reliable body of data are known as _____.
    a. vague notions.
    b. really good guesses.
    c. theories.
    d. hypotheses.
    e. factoids.

60. One may think of ethnology as the study of alternative ways of doing things. Moreover, by making systematic comparisons, ethnologists seek to arrive at scientific conclusions concerning the_____.
    a. healing traditions and practices.
    b. relationship between language and culture.
    c. function and operation of culture in all times and places.
    d. human evolution.
    e. enzymes, hormones, and other molecules.

61. The holy text believed to contain divine wisdom and eternal truths for Muslims is known as the _____.
    a. Torah.
    b. Koran.
    c. Bible.
    d. Webster's Dictionary.
    e. Encyclopedia Britannica.

62. The first African-American to become president of the American Anthropological Association was _____.
    a. Yolanda Moses
    b. Matilda Cox Stevenson.
    c. Margaret Mead.
    d. Ruth Benedict.
    e. Mahalia Jackson.

True/False Practice Questions

1. Culture is preserved and transmitted by language and observation.
   True or False

2. While ethnography is the in-depth study of a single culture, ethnology is the comparative study of culture.
   True or False

3. Ethnographic fieldwork is never done in Western societies.
   True or False

4. Anthropology can best be defined as the cross-cultural study of social behavior.
   True or False

5. Forensic anthropologists are particularly interested in the use of anthropological information for the purpose of debate, oratory and rhetorical criticism.
    True or False

6. A forensic anthropologist can even tell from skeletal remains whether the deceased was right or left handed.
    True or False

7. What a forensic anthropologist cannot tell from skeletal remains are details of an individual's health and nutritional history.
    True or False

8. Besides providing factual accounts of the fate of victims who had disappeared (*desparecidos*) to their surviving kin, Snow's work helped convict several Argentine military officers of kidnapping, torture, and murder.
    True or False

9. All cases of forensic anthropologists involve the abuse of police powers, and evidence provided by them is often ancillary to bringing the guilty party to justice.
    True or False

10. Franz Boas was the first to teach anthropology in the United States.
    True or False

11. Since the subject matter of anthropology is vast, a single anthropologist is personally able to investigate everything that has to do with people.
    True or False

12. Anthropologists know that if formulated correctly their theories will be completely beyond challenge.
    True or False

13. Archaeologists are cultural anthropologists.
    True or False

14. Ethnologists study languages throughout time to determine how they have changed.
    True or False

15. Anthropologists think of their findings as something apart from those of other social scientists.
    True or False

16. The subdisciplines of physical and cultural anthropology are closely related, since we cannot understand what people do unless we know what people are.
    True or False

17. Physical anthropologists just study fossil skulls, they would not be interested in studying the recently deceased.
    True or False

18. According to anthropological research, in North American society the ever-increasing amount of household appliance consumer goods has in fact resulted in a steady reduction in household work, with a consequent increase in leisure time.
    True or False

19. In a sense, one may think of ethnology as the study of alternative ways of doing things.
    True or False

20. No-where in the world have anthropologist documented same-sex marriages. In all human societies such unions are not deemed appropriate under any circumstances.
    True or False

21. Cultural and physical anthropologists share common interests in the interplay between human culture and biology.
    True or False

22. Because their differences are distributed independently, humans cannot be classified into races having any biological validity.
    True or False

23. According to your textbook, the violence triggered by East Timor's vote for independence exemplifies the problem of multinational states in which members of one nationality try to control those of another through all possible means.
    True or False

24. Anthropologists work within at least 10 subfields of the discipline of anthropology.
    True or False

25. Though each of the four subdisciplines of anthropology has its own research strategies, they rely upon each other and are united by a common anthropological perspective on the human condition.
    True or False

26. The main aim of anthropologists is to develop reliable theories about the human species.
    True or False

27. Linguistic anthropology focuses primarily on the cultural aspects of language, and as such has no connection with the discipline of physical anthropology.
    True or False

28. Biologically, humans are apes. That is, they are large bodied, broad shouldered primates with no tails.
    True or False

29. Detailed studies of the hormonal, genetic, and the physiological basis of healthy growth in living humans contributes only to our understanding of the growth patterns of our ancestors, and has nothing to do with the health of children today.
    True or False

30. Humans, because they differ from each other in many ways, can be categorized into several species.
    True or False

31. As long as a theory is widely accepted by the international community of scholars, it is beyond change.
    True or False

32. Generally, globalization has brought significant gains to higher-educated groups in wealthier countries, while doing little to boost developing countries and actually, contributing to the erosion of traditional cultures.
    True or False

33. In this age of globalization, anthropology may not only provide humanity with useful insights concerning diversity, but it may also assist us in avoiding or overcoming significant problems born of that diversity.
    True or False

34. Differences in skin color are simply surface adaptations to differing amounts of ultraviolet radiation and have nothing to do with physical or mental capabilities.
    True or False

35. Human "races" are nothing more than folk categories, and the sooner everyone recognizes that the categories lack scientific merit, the better off we will all be.
    True or False

36. Organ transplantation is merely a biological movement of an organ from one individual to another.
    True or False

Practice Matching

1. _____ Anthropology
2. _____ Physical anthropology
3. _____ Cultural anthropology
4. _____ Forensic anthropology
5. _____ Culture-bound
6. _____ Archaeology

a. Field of applied physical anthropology that specializes in the identification of human skeletal remains for legal purposes.
b. The systematic study of humans as biological organisms.
c. The study of humankind, in all times and places.
d. The branch of anthropology that focuses on human behavior.
e. The study of material remains, usually from the past, to describe and explain human behavior.
f. Theories about the world and reality based on the assumptions and values of one's own culture.

Practice Essays

1. Illustrate the usefulness of ethnographic fieldwork in North American society by discussing research on the theory of cultural deprivation among minority children.

2. Discuss the characteristics of participant-observation and how this method contributes to ethnographic understanding. How is this method characteristically different from other methods of social science research?

3. Describe how anthropology is, at the same time, a social/behavioral science, a natural science, and one of the humanities.

4. It was stated that it has been the office of other social sciences is to reassure; while the role of anthropology is to unsettle. Explain what is meant by this.

5. Your textbook gives three very different examples to illustrate the relevance of anthropological knowledge for the contemporary world. Identify and describe those examples.

6. Haviland asserts that anthropology is a kind of testing ground for the cross-cultural validity of disciplines like sociology, psychology, and economics, saying that it is to these disciplines what the laboratory is to physics and chemistry. What theory in another social science discipline can you think of that could usefully be tested cross-culturally?

7. Your textbook provides a rather lengthy discussion of the difficulties that arise in the application of the scientific approach in anthropology. What are the difficulties that arise when applying the scientific approach in anthropology?

8. How can a cultural practice affect human biology? Explain.

9. Who is Clyde Snow? Describe his work.

10. Haviland, the author of your textbook, used his own research to illustrate what he did to *do no harm* to the people who were the subject of his anthropological research. Describe what issues arose in his research and what he did to resolve them without doing any harm to his research subjects.

11. Describe the work of the various types of anthropologists.

12. Humans are the only species capable of studying themselves and the world around them. Explain why humans would want to study themselves.

13. Identify Suzanne Leclerc-Madlala and describe her research.

14. What is the difference between scientific theory and religious doctrine. Explain, using examples from your textbook.

15. Discuss the pros and cons of the issue of same sex marriage.

16. Providing examples, explain why the distinction between nation and state is important.

Solutions

Fill-in-the-Blank

1. culture
2. synthesize
3. biological
4. physical, cultural
5. forensic
6. material
7. ethnography
8. food foragers
9. hypothesis
10. slash-and-burn farming
11. Humanities
12. primates, Homo sapiens
13. biology
14. molecular anthropology
15. globalization
16. doctrine

Multiple-Choice Practice Questions

1. B
2. E
3. A
4. B
5. D
6. C
7. E
8. E
9. D
10. A
11. D
12. A
13. A
14. E
15. D
16. B
17. E
18. C
19. C
20. B
21. B
22. D
23. E
24. E
25. C
26. E
27. B
28. D
29. E
30. C
31. A
32. C
33. E
34. D
35. C
36. D
37. D
38. E
39. A
40. C
41. A
42. E
43. C
44. E
45. D
46. D
47. B
48. D
49. A
50. C
51. E
52. E
53. B
54. D
55. A
56. D
57. B
58. E
59. C
60. C
61. B
62. A

True/False Practice Questions

1. T
2. T
3. F
4. F
5. F
6. T
7. F
8. T
9. F
10. F
11. F
12. F

13. T		**5.** F	
14. F		**6.** E	
15. F			
16. T			
17. F			
18. F			
19. T			
20. F			
21. T			
22. T			
23. T			
24. F			
25. T			
26. T			
27. F			
28. T			
29. F			
30. F			
31. F			
32. T			
33. T			
34. T			
35. T			
36. F			

Practice Matching

1. C

2. B

3. D

4. A

Chapter 2

The Characteristics of Culture

Synopsis

In Chapter 2 the author considers the concept of culture, which underlies the anthropological enterprise. He proposes possible avenues for the definition of culture and describes how anthropologists attempt to study culture in the field. Finally, he raises questions as to whether it is possible for anthropologists to evaluate and compare cultures.

What You Should Learn from This Chapter

I.   Understand what culture is.

II.   Know how culture is transmitted along generations.

III.   Know how anthropologists conduct research into cultures.

IV.   Understand how culture functions in society.

V.   Understand the relationship between culture and adaptation.

Key Terms and Names

adaptation

cultural relativism

culture

enculturation

ethnocentrism

gender

pluralistic societies

social structure

society

structural-functionalism

subcultures

symbol

infrastructure

superstructure

Human Relations Area File (HRAF)

Ethnohistory

Exercise

Briefly identify the cultures listed below and locate them on the world map.

1.   Amish

2.   Kapauku Papuans

3.   Trobrianders

4.   Apache

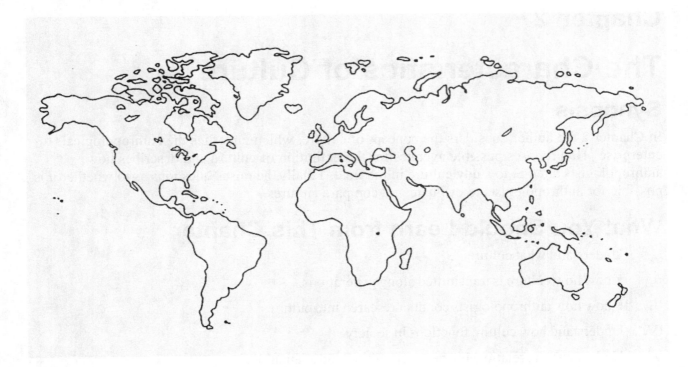

Exercise

Review Questions

1. What are four characteristics of culture, according to Haviland?

2. Distinguish between "culture" and "society." Do they always go together?

3. Distinguish between sex and gender.

4. Give an example of a pluralistic society, and consider what factors seem to allow the larger culture to tolerate subcultural variation.

5. How is culture passed on?

6. What is meant by the "integration" of various aspects of culture? Give an example.

7. How was anthropology able to contribute to the architectural problems of the Apache Indians?

8. What are three ways in which anthropologists should obtain data in another culture, according to the text?

9. How did Malinowski define the "needs" to be fulfilled by all cultures?

10. What did Annette Weiner find out about Trobriand women?

11. What five functions must a culture serve, according to your text?

12. What changes have recently impacted many pastoralists in sub-Saharan Africa?

13. In what ways must a balance be struck between society and the individuals who comprise it?

14. How can the large-scale sacrifices of the Aztec be explained?

15. Distinguish between ethnocentrism and cultural relativism.

16. According to Walter Goldschmidt, what aspects of society indicate how well the physical and psychological needs of its people are being met?

17. What was E.B. Tylor's original definition of culture in 1871? (This is a classic definition in anthropology, so it would be worthwhile to become familiar with it).

18. Approximately how old is human culture?

Fill-in-the-Blank

1. The culture concept was first developed in the _____ century.

2. Haviland defines culture as "a set of _____ shared by members of a society that when acted upon by the members of a society, produce behavior that falls withing a range of variance the members consider proper and acceptable."

3. When groups function within a society with their own distinctive standards of behavior, we speak of _____ variation.

4. Enculturation refers to the process through which culture is transmitted from one _____ to the next.

5. According to anthropologist _____ , all human behavior originates in the use of symbols.

6. Radcliffe-Brown was the originator of a school of thought known as _____ .

7. In Kapauku culture, gardens of _____ supply most of the food, but it is through breeding pigs that a man achieves political power.

8. There is a difference between what people say the rules are and actual behavior; that is, the anthropologist must distinguish between the _____ and the real.

9. Inheritance among the Trobrianders is carried through the _____ line.

10. Most organisms adapt by acquiring changes in their _____ .

11. Pastoral nomadic people in Africa south of the _____ have survived droughts because of their mobility.

12. The members of all societies consider their own culture to be the best; thus all people can be said to be _____ .

13. Anthropology tries to promote cultural _____ , or the idea that a culture must be evaluated according to its own standards.

Multiple-Choice Practice Questions

1. The contemporary definition of culture has changed from the meaning given to it during the nineteenth century. Today, _____.
   a. culture is seen as values and beliefs that lie behind behavior rather than as actual behavior.
   b. culture is seen as real rather than as ideal
   c. the term "culture" has been replaced by the term "society."
   d. culture is defined as objects rather than ideas
   e. the term "culture" is not used

2. One way to determine if people share the same culture is to observe whether they _____.
   a. are dependent on each other for survival
   b. are able to interpret and predict each other's actions
   c. live in the same territory
   d. behave in an identical manner
   e. "are dependent on each other for survival", "are able to interpret and predict each other's actions", "live in the same territory" and "behave in an identical manner"

3. Which of the following statements about society and culture is **incorrect**?
   a. Culture can exist without a society
   b. A society can exist without culture
   c. Ants and bees have societies but no culture
   d. A culture is shared by the members of a society
   e. Although members of a society may share a culture, their behavior is not uniform

4. Every culture teaches its members that there are differences between people based on sex, age, occupation, class, and ethnic group. People learn to predict the behavior of people playing different roles from their own. This means that _____.

   a. culture is shared even though everyone is not the same

   b. everyone plays the same role

   c. all cultures identify the same roles

   d. all cultures require that their participants play different roles, even though that means that no one can predict the behavior of others

   e. everyone plays the same role throughout his or her life

5. The cultural definitions of what it means to be a male or female today _____.

   a. are determined by biological differences

   b. are independent of biological differences

   c. stem from biological differences that today are relatively insignificant

   d. developed about 60 million years ago

   e. have no relationship to sex

6. When groups function within a society with their own distinctive standards of behavior, we speak of _____.

   a. subcultural variation

   b. social structure

   c. gender differences

   d. cultural materialism

   e. ethnocentrism

7. The Amish may be used as an example of a/an _____.

   a. pluralistic society

   b. subculture

   c. integrated society

   d. world culture

   e. complex society

8. The process by which culture is transmitted from one generation to the next is _____.

   a. enculturation

   b. pluralism

   c. adaptation

   d. cultural relativism

   e. subcultural variation

9. Which of the following statements is **incorrect**?

    a. All culture is learned

    b. All learned behavior is cultural

    c. Culture is humankind's "social heredity."

    d. Culture is not biologically inherited

    e. The process whereby culture is transmitted from one generation to the next is called enculturation

10. The most important symbolic aspect of culture is _____.

    a. art

    b. language

    c. religion

    d. money

    e. politics

11. Among the Kapauku Papuans of New Guinea, the fact that an attempt to eliminate warfare (Which would create a balanced sex ratio) would affect the practice of polygyny, which would affect the economy (since women raise pigs, and the more wives a man has the more pigs he can keep), shows that culture is _____.

    a. materialistic

    b. relative

    c. pluralistic

    d. integrated

    e. enculturated

12. An anthropologist develops a concept of culture by considering which of the following sources of data from the field?

    a. what people say they ought to do

    b. how people think they are behaving in accordance with these rules

    c. what people actually do

    d. "what people say they ought to do", "how people think they are behaving in accordance with these rules" and "what people actually do"

    e. none of these

13. When Annette Weiner went to the Trobriand Islands sixty years after Malinowski had been there, she found that _____.

    a. the culture had changed so much that it was almost unrecognizable

    b. Malinowski's views of wealth, political power, and descent were primarily from the male's point of view

    c. Malinowski had attributed power to women that did not exist

    d. only women were significant producers of wealth

    e. women played no role in producing wealth

14. The process by which organisms adjust beneficially to their environment, or the characteristics by which they overcome hazards and gain access to the resources they need to survive, is called _____.
    a. culture
    b. biology
    c. social structure
    d. integration
    e. adaptation

15. Behavior can be adaptive in the short run but maladaptive in the long run. In the Central Valley in California, vast irrigation projects have created a garden, but salts and chemicals accumulating in the soil will eventually create another desert. This same process occurred in _____.
    a. Mexico
    b. Morocco
    c. ancient Mesopotamia
    d. Great Britain
    e. the Yellow River valley of China

16. A culture must satisfy basic needs such as _____.
    a. the distribution of necessary goods and services
    b. biological continuity through reproduction and enculturation of functioning adults
    c. maintenance of order within a society and between a society and outsiders
    d. motivation to survive
    e. "the distribution of necessary goods and services", "biological continuity through reproduction and enculturation of functioning adults", "maintenance of order within a society and between a society and outsiders" and "motivation to survive"

17. _____ refers to the position that because cultures are unique, each one should be evaluated according to its own standards and values.
    a. Ethnocentrism
    b. Cultural relativism
    c. Cultural materialism
    d. Adaptation
    e. Pluralism

18. Goldschmidt suggests that it is possible to decide which cultures are more successful than others by looking at which ones _____.
    a. survive
    b. last the longest
    c. satisfy the physical and cultural needs of the people
    d. support the most people
    e. are the least emotional

19. A mountain people of western New Guinea studied in 1955 by the North American anthropologist Leo Pospisil.

    a. !Kung San

    b. Kaluli

    c. Basseri

    d. Kapauku

    e. Azande

20. We now know that any culture that is functioning adequately regards itself as the best, a view reflecting a phenomenon known as _____.

    a. cultural relativism

    b. egoism

    c. nationalisti

    d. ethnocentrism

    e. individualism

21. The idea that one must suspend judgement on other peoples' practices in order to understand them in their own cultural terms is called _____.

    a. structuralism

    b. functionalism

    c. structural functionalism

    d. cultural relativism

    e. relative culturalism

22. In regards to the concept of cultural relativism, anthropologist _____ emphasized that "...one does not avoid making judgements, but rather postpones them in order to make informed judgements later."

    a. David Maybury-Lewis

    b. Daniel Day-Lewis

    c. Francis L.K. Shu

    d. E.E. Evans-Pritchard

    e. A.F.C. Wallace

23. As a result of _____ work, in 1981, the Apaches were able to move into houses that had been designed with their participation, for their specific needs.

    a. Walter Goldschmidt's

    b. George Esber's

    c. David Maybury-Lewis's

    d. Bronislaw Kasper Malinowski's

    e. Margaret Mead's

24. The British anthropologist _____ was the originator of what has come to be known as the structural-functionalist school of thought.
    a. Claude Levi-Strauss
    b. George Simmel
    c. A.R. Radcliffe-Brown
    d. Leslie A. White
    e. Ruth Benedict

25. _____ was a major theoretician in North American anthropology who saw culture as consisting of three essential components, which he referred to as techno-economic, the social, and the ideological.
    a. A.R. Radcliffe-Brown
    b. Leslie A. White
    c. Leopold Pospisil
    d. A.B. Weiner
    e. William Jankowiak

26. To insure survival of a group of people, a culture must do which of the following?
    a. satisfy the basic needs of those who live by its rules
    b. provide for its own continuity
    c. provide an orderly existence for members of a society
    d. have the capacity to change
    e. "satisfy the basic needs of those who live by its rules", "provide for its own continuity", "provide an orderly existence for members of a society" and "have the capacity to change"

27. To answer such questions as: why do particular customs arise in the first place, and how do cultures change? _____ approaches are necessary.
    a. Structural
    b. Functional
    c. Historical
    d. Mechanical
    e. Structural-functional

28. In 1871, _____ defined culture as "that complex whole which includes knowledge, belief, art, law, morals, custom and any other capabilities and habits acquired by man as a member of society.
    a. A.L. Kroeber
    b. Clyde Kluckhohn
    c. Edward Burnett Taylor
    d. Karl Marx
    e. Margaret Mead

29. Which of the following is **not** a characteristic of society?
    a. A group of people who share a common homeland
    b. A group of people who are dependent on each other for survival
    c. A group of people who share a culture
    d. A group of people who share a common identity
    e. All are characteristic of a society; "A group of people who share a common homeland", "A group of people who are dependent on each other for survival", "A group of people who share a culture" and "A group of people who share a common identity"

30. To survive, a culture must _____.
    a. satisfy the basic needs of those who live by its rules
    b. provide for its own continuity
    c. furnish an orderly existence for the members of its society
    d. strike a balance between the self-interests of individuals and the needs of society as a whole
    e. "satisfy the basic needs of those who live by its rules", "provide for its own continuity", "furnish an orderly existence for the members of its society" and "strike a balance between the self-interests of individuals and the needs of society as a whole"

31. Gender differences are as old as human culture, or about _____ years.
    a. 5 million
    b. 2.5 million
    c. 100,000
    d. 250,000
    e. 1 million

32. The thesis that one must suspend judgment on other peoples' practices to understand them in their own cultural terms.
    a. Ethnocentrism
    b. Separatism
    c. Social relativism
    d. Socialism
    e. Cultural relativism

33. The job of anthropologists is to abstract a set of rules from what they observe to explain the social behavior of a people. To arrive at a realistic description of a culture free from personal and cultural biases, anthropologists must _____.
    a. based on the anthropologists' culture, make judgements on other peoples' practices to understand them
    b. examine a people's notion of the way their society ought to function
    c. determine how a people think they behave
    d. compare how people think they ought to behave with how they actually behave
    e. "examine a people's notion of the way their society ought to function", "determine how a people think they behave", "compare how people think they ought to behave with how they actually behave"

34. Although citizens of the United States are fond of boasting that theirs is the finest health care system in the world, they are merely reflecting _____ of their own culture.
    a. nationalism
    b. eclecticism
    c. ethnocentrism
    d. relativism
    e. euphemism

35. Through culture, the human species has secured not just its survival but its expansion. Which of the following would be examples of human expansion?
    a. settlements in the Arctic region
    b. flights to the moon
    c. settlements in the Sahara Desert
    d. the exploration of space
    e. "settlements in the Arctic region", "flights to the moon", "settlements in the Sahara Desert" and "the exploration of space"

36. Because subsistence practices involve tapping into available resources to satisfy a society's basic needs, this aspect of culture is known as_____.
    a. infrastructure.
    b. subculture
    c. social structure
    d. superstructure.
    e. acculturation.

37. The initiator of the Human Relations Area File (HRAF) was _____ at Yale University.
    a. Eleanor Leacock
    b. George Peter Murdock
    c. Leslie White
    d. A.R. Radcliffe-Brown
    e. Bronislaw Malinowski

38. A pioneer in feminist anthropology, _____ was among the first to critically examine anthropological writings from a woman's perspective.
    a. Margaret Mead
    b. Ruth Benedict
    c. Eleanor Burke Leacock
    d. Annette Weiner
    e. Barbara Roth

True/False Practice Questions

1. To say that culture is shared means that all members of a society behave in the same way.
   True or False

2. A pluralistic society always has subcultural variation, but not every society with subcultural variation is pluralistic.
   True or False

3. A larger culture is more likely to tolerate a subculture if their values and physical appearances are similar.
   True or False

4. Cattle herding is the mainstay around which all of Kapauku Papuan society revolves.
   True or False

5. A modern definition of culture emphasizes the values, beliefs, and rules that lie behind behavior rather than the actual observable behavior itself.
   True or False

6. Gender differences were more extreme among food foragers than among late nineteenth and early twentieth century Westerners.
   True or False

7. Annette Weiner agrees that ethnographic writing can never be more than a fictional account.
   True or False

8. There are some societies that have no regulation of sex whatsoever.
   True or False

9. There can be no culture without a society.
   True or False

10. Ants and bees instinctively cooperate in a manner that clearly indicates a degree of social organization, therefore they have culture.
    True or False

11. Though one's sex is culturally determined, one's sexual identity or gender is biologically constructed.
    True or False

12. The degree of tolerance accorded the Amish is due in part to the fact that they are "white" Europeans.
    True or False

13. So-called racial characteristics represent biological adaptations to climate and have nothing to do with differences in intelligence or cultural superiority.
    True or False

14. Learned behavior is exhibited to one degree or another by most, if not all, mammals.
    True or False

15. If a society is to survive it must succeed in balancing the self-interest of its members against the demands of the society as a whole.
    True or False

16. Numerous studies by a variety of social scientists have clearly shown that the death penalty does deter violent crime in the United States.
    True or False

17. Cross cultural studies show that homicide rates mostly decline after the death penalty is abolished.
True or False

18. Universally, individuals are regarded as adults when they reach the age of eighteen.
True or False

19. People maintain cultures to deal with problems or matters that concern them.
True or False

20. A culture must have the capacity to change so it can adapt to altered perceptions of existing circumstances.
True or False

21. Cultures are biologically inherited, rather than learned.
True or False

22. Humans do everything because it is adaptive to a particular environment.
True or False

23. What is adaptive in one context may be seriously maladaptive in another.
True or False

24. The tricks that pigeons learn are the product of enculturation.
True or False

25. For a culture to function properly, its various parts must be consistent with each other because consistency means harmony.
True or False

26. HRAF is a valuable research tool that not only allows anthropologists to establish correlations between cultural features, but also permits conclusions about cause and effect.
True or False

27. Anthropologists seldom look at the archaeological or historical record to test hypotheses about culture change.
True or False

Practice Matching

Match the culture with its description.

1. _____ Amish
2. _____ Trobrianders
3. _____ Kapauku Papuans
4. _____ Aztec
5. _____ Apache

a. A Native American people with distinct architectural needs.
b. A Pacific Island people studied by both Malinowski and Weiner.
c. A pacifist agrarian subculture of the U.S.
d. A New Guinea people who breed pigs.
e. A civilization in Mexico that engaged in large-scale sacrifices.

Short Answer

1. What must be done for a culture to function properly?

2. What is meant by the statement "culture is dynamic?"

3. What happens when a culture is too rigid?

4. Ethnohistorical research is valuable for testing hypotheses about culture. However, it has a practical use as well. What is the practical use of ethnohistorical research?

5. Although people maintain cultures to deal with problems, it is clear that some cultural practices prove to be maladaptive and actually create new problems. Provide examples of cultural practices that have proved maladaptive, creating new problems.

6. In anthropology, what is Eleanor Burke Leacock's claim to fame?

7. Are animals other than humans capable of culture?

8. Explain why people maintain cultures?

9. What is the purpose of the Human Relations Area Files?

Practice Essays

1. Using the Amish as an example of subcultural variation, discuss some of the factors that seem to determine whether or not subcultural variation is tolerated by the larger culture. Compare the Amish to another group that is less well-tolerated.

2. Distinguish between the concepts of culture and society.

3. Discuss the distinction between sex and gender and explain why this distinction is important.

4. Discuss the interrelatedness of the various parts of Kapauku culture. Use examples.

5. Because of the male bias of his European culture, Bronislaw Malinowski's pioneering study of the Trobriand Islanders missed many important factors. Discuss the factors that were overlooked due to male bias.

6. Provide examples to support the statement, "What is adaptive in one context may be seriously maladaptive in another."

7. Using the example of the Kapauku Papuans, explain the idea that culture is integrated.

8. Anthropologist James Peacock wrote a book called The *Anthropological Lens* in which he compared culture to a lens or glass through which people experience the world. The anthropologist, then, is like an oculist who hopes to find the "formula" of each kind of lens, acquiring a kind of stereoscopy, or depth perception, by being able to perceive things through multiple lenses. How is culture like a lens? What are the limitations of this metaphor for understanding culture and anthropology?

9. Discuss how one's gender might impact one's research findings.

Solutions

Fill-in-the-Blank

1. 19th
2. shared ideals, values, and standards of behavior
3. subcultural
4. generation
5. Leslie White
6. structural functionalism
7. sweet potatoes
8. ideal
9. matrilineal
10. bodies
11. Sahara
12. ethnocentric
13. relativity

Multiple-Choice Practice Questions

1. A
2. B
3. A
4. A
5. C
6. A
7. B
8. A
9. B
10. B
11. D
12. D
13. B
14. E
15. C
16. E
17. B
18. C
19. D
20. D
21. D
22. A
23. B
24. C
25. B
26. E
27. C
28. C
29. E
30. E
31. B
32. E
33. E
34. C
35. E
36. A
37. B
38. C

True/False Practice Questions

1. F
2. T
3. T
4. F
5. T
6. F
7. F
8. F
9. T
10. F
11. F
12. T
13. T
14. T
15. T
16. F
17. T
18. F
19. T
20. T
21. F
22. F
23. T
24. F
25. T
26. F
27. F

Practice Matching

1. C
2. B
3. D
4. E
5. A

Chapter 3

The Beginnings of Human Culture

Synopsis

Culture evolved as the primary adaptation of our species over millions of years. In this chapter Haviland traces the intertwining of biological and cultural evolution through the history of our fossil ancestors, looking at major milestones like the development of stone tools, the first use of fire, the rise of cooperative hunting, and language as a means of communication. And finally, this chapter looks at the concept of race and its utility for the study of physical variation in the human species.

What You Should Learn from This Chapter

I.   Understand that culture is our species= major mode of adaptation.

II.   Know the major fossil ancestors of our species and approximately where and when they lived.

III.   Understand the biological changes that led to the current physical structure of our species.

IV.   Know what the major milestones in the development of culture were, and approximately where and when they occurred.

V.   Understand how the study of human evolution complements and enhances the study of the diversity of cultures today.

Key Terms

Adaptation
Ardipithecus
Australopithecus
Bipedalism
Frans de Waal
Hominoids
Homo erectus
Homo habilis
Homo sapiens
Jane Goodall
Kinji Imanishi
Lower Paleolithic

Mousterian
Multiregional hypothesis
natural selection
Neandertals
Oldowan
Paleoanthropologists
Primatologists
Race
Recent African origins
primate order
Upper Paleolithic

Exercise

Review Questions

1. To what biological order do humans belong? What other kinds of animals belong to this order?

2. Describe the environment to which early primates adapted through natural selection.

3. What are the distinguishing features of the primates?

4. In what ways can apes adapt to their environment through learning?

5. Why is dentition important to the study of human evolution?

6. Under what conditions might bipedalism have emerged?

7. What features of *Australopithecus* were more humanlike, and what features were more apelike?

8. What was the Aprotein problem@ faced by evolving primates? How was it resolved?

9. When and where did the first stone tools appear? What were they like?

10. How did the appearance of stone tools relate to changes in brain size, teeth, and diet?

11. How did the different roles played by males and females in the search for food affect selection for intelligence in early *Homo* ?

12. What was the geographical distribution of *Homo erectus*? What were its physical characteristics?

13. What was the impact of the use of fire on our fossil ancestors?

14. What other cultural developments took place during *Homo erectus* times?

15. What is the difference between a hominine and a hominoid?

16. What is the role played by grooming in primate social order?

17. When did *Homo sapiens* first appear? What were its characteristics?

18. What is the African origins, also know as the Eve or out of Africa hypothesis? What is the evidence for and against it?

19. What was the tool-making tradition of the Neandertals?

20. In what other ways did culture develop in Neandertal times?

21. What were the major cultural developments of the Upper Paleolithic?

22. How did the notion of distinct human races come to be?

23. Why don't anthropologists consider race to be a valid biological category?

24. What is the significance of race as a social category in the United States?

Fill-in-the-Blank

1. Humans belong to the _____ Order, along with lemurs, indriids, lorises, tarsiers, monkeys, and apes.

2. Primates have fewer and less _____ teeth in comparison to the ancestral animals from which they evolved.

3. The senses that are highly developed in primates are _____ , touch, and smell.

4. The tree-dwelling environment to which early primates adapted is called an _____ habitat.

5. The depth perception characteristic of primates stems from their _____ vision.

6. Instead of claws, most primates have _____ .

7. Primate brains are large, especially the _____ hemispheres.

8. A behavior of primates that encourages social bonding is _____ .

9. Jane Goodall carried out a long-term study of chimpanzees in _____ .

10. The first hominine to walk fully upright was _____ .

11. Walking on two legs is called _____ .

12. A new find that may represent the earliest form of *Australopithecus* is _____ .

13. The earliest stone tools are about _____ million years old.

14. It was *Homo* _____ who made Oldowan tools.

15. *Homo erectus* spread beyond Africa to _____ .

16. Neandertal tool-making traditions are called _____ .

17. The _____ hypothesis suggests that all modern humans are derived from a single population of archaic *H. sapiens*.

18. Upper Paleolithic peoples spread into two new geographic areas: _____ and _____ .

19. _____ is a social construct that varies from culture to culture.

20. _____ appear in continuous gradations from one population to another without sharp breaks.

Multiple-Choice Practice Questions

1. On the cave wall at **Grotte de Chauvet**, France is a painting that provides tangible proof of the human ability to create cultural symbols. The cave painting was done _____ years ago during the last ice age.
   a. 100,000
   b. 32,000
   c. 55,000
   d. 15,000
   e. 22,000

2. _____ was the first change to distinguish the human evolutionary line from that of other primates.
   a. An acute sense of smell
   b. Sharpened visual acuity
   c. Bipedalism
   d. The prehensile tail
   e. Increased tactile sensitivity

3. Present evidence suggests that humans evolved from small, African apes between _____ and _____ million years ago.
   a. 10/15
   b. 1/4
   c. 12/20
   d. 5/8
   e. 50/100

4. Anthropologists have actively worked to get rid of race as a biological category while recognizing the significance of race as a social category in which of the following cultures?

    a. Brazil

    b. Puerto Rico

    c. The United States

    d. South Africa

    e. C and D

5. _____ study human evolutionary history.

    a. Molecular anthropologists

    b. Primatologists

    c. Paleoanthropologists

    d. Ethnologists

    e. Biologists

6. _____ study living primates.

    a. Physiologists

    b. Ethnographers

    c. Paleoanthropologists

    d. Primatologists

    e. Zoologists

7. At times evolution occurs through a process known as_____, a series of beneficial adjustments of organisms to their environment.

    a. adaptation

    b. natural selection

    c. assimilation

    d. acculturation

    e. accomodation

8. Evolution by _____ refers to differences in survival and reproduction among individuals leading to a change in a species over time as the species adapts to its environment.

    a. adaptation

    b. natural selection

    c. accomodation

    d. acculturation

    e. assimilation

9. Individuals who grow up in very cold climates develop certain circulatory system features to keep their hands and feet warm despite cold environmental temperatures. These changes in the body are known as_____.

    a. cultural adaptations.

    b. physiological adaptations.

    c. developmental adaptations.

    d. natural selection.

    e. environmental accommodations.

10. Humans are capable of short term _____to the environment such as shivering to produce heat, or producing more red blood cells to carry oxygen at higher altitudes.

    a. cultural adaptations

    b. physiological adaptations

    c. developmental adaptations

    d. natural selection

    e. environmental accomodations

11. Humans are unique in their biological capacity to produce a rich array of_____to the environment.

    a. cultural adaptations.

    b. physiological adaptations.

    c. natural selection.

    d. environmental accommodations.

    e. developmental attibutes.

12. The fundamental elements of human culture came into existence a mere _____million years ago.

    a. 1

    b. 3.6

    c. 2.5

    d. 100

    e. 25

13. With the benefit of detailed field studies over the last thirty years, many of which were pioneered by female primatologists like_____, the nuances of primate social behavior and the importance of female primates has been documented.

    a. Jennifer Thompson

    b. Ruth Benedict

    c. Margaret Mead

    d. Jane Goodall

    e. Laura Nader

14. Noted Japanese primatologist,_____, developed a harmonious theory of evolution and initiated field studies of bonobos that have shown the importance of social cooperation rather than competition.

    a. Bob Fujigawa

    b. Tsushiro Mifume

    c. Roy Ogawa

    d. Lisa Fujinaga

    e. Imanishi Kinji

15. Microscopic analysis of cut marks on bones has revealed that the earliest members of the genus *Homo* were not hunters but_____.

    a. trackers.

    b. fierce warriors.

    c. tertiary scavengers.

    d. secondary scavengers.

    e. trappers.

16. The fossil record is particularly rich when it comes to_____, perhaps the most notorious member of the genus *Homo*.

    a. Ardipithecus ramidus

    b. Neandertal

    c. Australopithecus

    d. Homo habilis

    e. Homo sapien

17. Both the Multiregional Hypothesis and the Recent African Origins theories place human origins firmly in_____.

    a. China.

    b. Australia.

    c. Africa.

    d. Europe.

    e. North America.

18. By the early 20th century _____ the father of American anthropology, was one of the first to challenge hierarchical notions of race.

    a. Johann Blumenbach

    b. Ashley Montegu

    c. Franz Boas

    d. Bronislaw Malinowski

    e. Clyde Snow

19. _____'s book *Man's Most Dangerous Myth: The Fallacy of Race* was published in 1942. That book scientifically exposed the fallacy of human races as biological entities.

    a. Ashley Montegu

    b. Johann Blumenbach

    c. Franz Boas

    d. Claude Levi-Strauss

    e. A.R. Radcliffe-Brown

20. Anthropologist_____suggests that the downward trajectory for human health began with the earliest human settlements some 10,000 years ago.

    a. Jennifer Thompson

    b. Bernardo Arriaza

    c. George Armelagos

    d. Ashley Montegu

    e. Ruth Benedict

21. _____, the basic inheritable building blocks, determine the biological traits and characteristics of each individual.

    a. phonemes

    b. proteins

    c. genes

    d. alleles

    e. sperm

22. Compared to the _____ billion year history of the earth, humans have gotten where they are today in an extraordinary short period of time.

    a. 10.1

    b. 7.3

    c. 75.5

    d. 4.6

    e. 6.4

23. Biologists classify humans as_____.

    a. Homo erectus.

    b. Homo habilis.

    c. Ardipithecus..

    d. Australopithecus.

    e. Homo sapien..

24. Biologists classify humans as members of the_____order.
    a. Primate
    b. Sacred
    c. Major
    d. Homologic
    e. Platyrrhini

25. Humans are classified as members of the subgroup_____.
    a. Primate.
    b. Mammals.
    c. Haplorhini
    d. Platyrrhini
    e. Australopithecine.

26. Biological _____are defined by reproductive isolation, or the ability to interbreed and produce live, fertile offspring.
    a. orders
    b. subgroups
    c. genus
    d. species
    e. adaptations

27. Evidence from ancient skeletal material indicates that the first mammals appeared as small, _____or nighttime creatures over 200 million years ago.
    a. diurnal
    b. diachronic
    c. synchronic
    d. nocturnal
    e. subterraneum

28. Today most species are _____ or active during the day.
    a. diurnal
    b. chronomatic
    c. nocturnal
    d. polytypic
    e. arboreal

29. The earliest primate creatures evolved approximately _____ million years ago.
    a. 200
    b. 75
    c. 65
    d. 100
    e. 25

30. The varied diet available to _____or tree dwelling primates, i.e., shoots, leaves, insects, and fruits, did not require specializations of the teeth seen in other animals.

    a.   arboreal

    b.   nocturnal

    c.   diurnal

    d.   primoreal

    e.   Catarrhini

True/False Practice Questions

1.   The environment selected for the distinctive characteristics of the primate order was arboreal.
     True or False

2.   Chimpanzees and bonobos have been observed to hunt cooperatively and to share meat.
     True or False

3.   *Homo habilis* learned how to use fire at the same time as it developed Oldowan tools.
     True or False

4.   Hominines became bipedal at about the same time as their brain size radically increased.
     True or False

5.   There is some dispute about the relationship between the Neanderthal and ourselves.
     True or False

6.   According to Haviland, the chimpanzees and bonobos represent a accurate model for the behavior of our own ancient ancestors.
     True or False

7.   Chimpanzees and bonobos are the most skilled of the apes in manipulating objects.
     True or False

8.   The biological concept of race is useful for studying physical variation in the human species.
     True or False

9.   Since races are arbitrarily defined, the division of humans into discrete types does not represent the true nature of human variation, therefore the biological concept of race is not useful for studying physical variation in the human species.
     True or False

10. Evolution does not allow for chance or random events to contribute to biological change through time.
     True or False

11. Human populations are genetically open, which means genes flow between them. As such no fixed racial groups can exist.
     True or False

12. Given what we know about the adaptive significance of human skin color, and the fact that, until 800,000 years ago, members of the genus Homo were exclusively creatures of the tropics, it is likely that darkly pigmented skins are a recent development in human history.
     True or False

13. Lightly pigmented skin color is likely an ancient development.
    True or False

14. All humans appear to have had a Black ancestry, no matter how White some of them appear today.
    True or False

15. From a biological perspective culture has rendered skin color differences largely irrelevant.
    True or False

16. No living primate represents a precise analogue for the behavior of our own ancient ancestors.
    True or False

17. Among chimps, all offspring are fathered by dominant males.
    True or False

18. In most primate species, females and their offspring constitute the core of the social system.
    True or False

19. Anatomical adaptation is important to primates because it is the only way they have of coping with the environment.
    True or False

20. Sexual activity among chimpanzees and bonobos occurs only during the period of each month when the female is fertile.
    True or False

21. Chimpanzees and bonobos are strictly vegetarians. They refrain from eating any meat.
    True or False

22. The most sophisticated example of teamwork in hunting occurs among the orangutan.
    True or False

Practice Essays

1. If you had to pick three to six key developments in the evolution of culture, what would they be? Write an essay identifying their importance to culture as we know among human beings.

2. What one question do you feel remains unanswered about the evolution of humans and human culture? That is, if you could make one key discovery, what would it be? Why would it be critical to our understanding of evolution?

3. From the study of both ancient and modern primates, anthropologists have worked out a list of anatomical characteristics common to them all. Identify those characteristics and explain how each facilitated the adaptation to an arboreal environment.

4. Compare and contrast the behavior of chimpanzees and bonobos, the closest genetic relatives to humans.

5. Describe chimpanzee patterns of behavior and discuss how they might have contributed to the emergence of human cultural behavior.

6. There are two major theories regarding the evolution of modern *H. sapiens*. Identify, compare, and contrast those two theories.

7. Discuss the significance of meat eating and stone tool making for human evolution.

8. Discuss the importance of gathering in the evolution of human culture. Whose responsibility was gathering? What carrying devices were invented to gather foodstuff. These early carry devices evolved into some modern carrying devices. Identify and discuss the evolution of carrying devices that are in use today.

9. Important though anatomical adaptation has been to the primates, it has not been the only way primates have coped with their environment. Using examples, describe other ways primates have adapted to their environment?

10. Evidence indicates that at least one population of archaic *Homo sapiens* evolved into modern humans. Identify that population and describe what made them different from earlier forms of the genus *Homo.*

11. Explain why the racial approach to human variation has been so unproductive and damaging, and why Arace as a biological concept is flawed.

12. Discuss the adaptive significance of human skin color.

13. Who is Imanishi Kinji and how did his research challenge western evolutionary theory?

14. Though increased life expectancy is often hailed as one of modern civilization's greatest accomplishments, in some ways today's humans lead far less healthy lifestyles than their ancestors. In what ways are contemporary lifestyles less healthy than those of our ancestors? Describe and explain.

Solutions

Fill-in-the-Blank

1. Primate
2. specialized
3. vision
4. arboreal
5. Stereoscopic
6. Flexible digits
7. cerebral
8. grooming
9. Tanzania
10.
11. bipedal
12.
13. 2.5
14.
15. Europe and Asia
16. Mousterian
17. "Out-of-Africa"
18. Australia, the Americas
19. Race
20. Differences that exist among populations

Multiple-Choice Practice Questions

1. B
2. C
3. D
4. E
5. C
6. D
7. A
8. B
9. C
10. B
11. A
12. C
13. D
14. E
15. C
16. B
17. C
18. C
19. A
20. C
21. C
22. D
23. E
24. A
25. B
26. D
27. D
28. A
29. C
30. B

True/False Practice Questions

1. T
2. T
3. F
4. F
5. T
6. F
7. F
8. F
9. T
10. F
11. T
12. F
13. F
14. T
15. T
16. T
17. F
18. T
19. F
20. T
21. F
22. F

Chapter 4

Language and Communication

Synopsis

Chapter 4 introduces the field of anthropological linguistics, considering how existing languages are described and studied and what the history of language can tell us. It examines how language is related to culture and explores the evolution of the capacity for language. An extensive technical vocabulary relating to linguistics is presented.

What You Should Learn from This Chapter

I.   Know how humans communicate with one another.

II.   Know what linguistics is and the components of language.

III. Understand how humans use paralanguage to communicate.

IV.   Understand how humans use kinesics to communicate.

V.   Know how ethnolinguistics aids in understanding culture.

VI.   Know the explanations offered about the origin of language.

Key Terms

alphabet
bound morphemes
code switching
core vocabulary
dialects
descriptive linguistics
displacement
ethnolinguistics
form classes
frame substitution
free morpheme
gendered speech
glottochronology
grammar
historical linguistics
kinesics
language
language family
linguistic divergence
linguistic nationalism
linguistic relativity

linguistics
morphemes
morphology
paralanguage
phonemes
phonetic
phonology
pidgin
proxemics
signal
sociolinguistics
symbol
syntax
theory of linguistic relativity
vocal characterizers
vocal qualifiers
vocal segregates
vocalizations
voice qualities
writing system

Exercise

Review Questions

1. Why is language so important to culture?

2. What is the anatomical "price we pay" for our vocal capabilities?

3. What does primatologist Allison Jolly mean by the "audience effect" she observes among the primates she studies?

4. Distinguish between a morpheme and a phoneme and give an example of each.

5. Distinguish between bound and free morphemes and give examples of each.

6. What is the function of frame substitution?

7. What is the purpose of a form class?

8. What method does descriptive linguistics use?

9. What is paralanguage? Provide examples.

10. What are the characteristic differences in body posture between men and women?

11. What is the "gesture-call" system?

12. What are the elements of voice quality?

13. Distinguish between vocal characterizers and vocal qualifiers.

14. How are gender markers employed?

15. What is code switching? Give an example you have observed.

16. What does glottochronology seek to explain?

17. Describe the importance of language for group identity.

18. What does ethnolinguistics seek to explain?

19. Provide an example that would support the theory of linguistic relativity.

20. What is meant by color-naming behavior?

21. How can linguists use metaphor as a key to understanding culture?

22. Why do linguists study kinship terms?

23. Haviland notes that wild speculation about the origins of language is no longer necessary. What advances have been made that make such speculation unnecessary?

24. What types of communication have primates been taught?

25. What are the communicative capabilities of monkeys and apes?

26. What is the difference between a signal and a symbol?

Fill-in-the-Blank

1. There are about _____ languages in the world.

2. A symbol has an arbitrary meaning determined by cultural convention, while a _____ has a natural or self-evident meaning.

3. Of all the potential sounds that can be made by the human vocal system, no more than _____ are used by any particular language.

4. The modern scientific study of language by Europeans began in the _____ with the collection of information about exotic languages by European explorers, invaders, and missionaries.

5. _____ is the systematic study of the production, transmission, and reception of speech sounds.

6. The smallest class of sound that makes a difference in meaning is called a _____ .

7. The smallest significant unit of sound that carries a meaning is called a _____ .

8. The entire formal structure of a language is called its _____ .

9. The method used to define the rules and regularities of a language is called frame _____ .

10. _____ refers to the extralinguistic noises that accompany language.

11. Voice _____ are the background characteristics of a speaker's voice that convey the state of the speaker.

12. Sounds such as "shh" and "uh-huh" that are similar to speech sounds but do not appear in sequences that can be called words are vocal _____ .

13. _____ is usually referred to as "body language."

14. _____ linguistics studies relationships between earlier and later languages.

15. English belongs to the _____ language family.

16. Linguistic _____ refers to the attempt by nations to proclaim their independence and and distinctive identity by celebrating their own language.

17. The study of the relationship between language and social factors is called _____ .

18. The process by which a person changes from one level of language to another is called _____ .

Multiple-Choice Practice Questions

1. A system of communication based on symbols is called a _____.

    a. signal

    b. form class

    c. language

    d. frame substitution

    e. vocalization

2. All languages are organized on the same basic plan in that _____.

    a. they are all based on signals

    b. they take no more than fifty sounds and put them together in meaningful ways according to rules that can be determined by linguists.

    c. they take no more than three thousand sounds and organize them according to the rules of grammar

    d. they all evolved from a common Egyptian language

    e. they originated in Russia

3. The modern scientific study of all aspects of language is _____.
   a. kinesics
   b. phonology
   c. linguistics
   d. grammar
   e. glottochronology

4. The systematic study of the production, transmission, and reception of speech sounds is _____.
   a. linguistics
   b. morphology
   c. frame substitution
   d. phonetics
   e. syntax

5. Paralanguage is to speech as _____ is to position of the body.
   a. kinesics
   b. ethnolinguistics
   c. form class
   d. phonetics
   e. displacement

6. Consider the English word "dog." Which of the following is a morpheme?
   a. "d"
   b. "dog"
   c. "o"
   d. "g"
   e. "d", "dog","o" and "g"

7. The sounds s and z in "cats" and "dogs" are examples of _____.
   a. allophones
   b. allomorphs
   c. free morphemes
   d. bound morphemes
   e. signals

8. The method called frame substitution enables the linguist to establish the rules or principles by which language users construct phrases and sentences, that is, the _____ of the language.
   a. morphology
   b. form classes
   c. core vocabulary
   d. sociolinguistics
   e. syntax

9. Two people say to you, "You sure look nice today." Although they are saying the same words, you can tell that one person is being complimentary and the other sarcastic by their _____.

    a. vocalizations

    b. vocal characteristics

    c. voice qualities

    d. voice segregates

    e. vocal qualifiers

10. Kinesics is a method for notating and analyzing _____.

    a. screaming

    b. kissing

    c. any form of body 'language.'

    d. fighting

    e. food

11. Descriptive linguistics _____.

    a. attempts to explain the features of a particular language at one time in its history

    b. looks at languages as separate systems without considering how they might be related to each other

    c. attempts to construct a language's historical development

    d. investigates relationships between earlier and later forms of the same language

    e. "attempts to explain the features of a particular language at one time in its history" and "looks at languages as separate systems without considering how they might be related to each other"

12. A language family is a group of languages that _____.

    a. all have the same core vocabulary

    b. are subordinate to a dominant language

    c. all have the same syntax

    d. use the same number of sounds

    e. are descended from a single ancestral language

13. If the core vocabulary of two languages is compared by glottochronologists, it is thought possible to determine _____.

    a. if the two languages perceive reality in the same way

    b. if the two languages use the same syntax

    c. if they share the same allophones

    d. if they have a similar technology

    e. how long ago the languages separated from each other

14. Which of the following statements about linguistic divergence is **incorrect**?

    a. One force for linguistic change is borrowing by one language from another

    b. If languages were isolated from each other, there would be very little linguistic change

    c. New vocabulary emerges in a language due to quest for novelty and the development of specialized vocabulary by groups

    d. Changes in pronunciation may emerge as markers of class boundary (e.g., upper-class"U" versus "Non-U")

    e. Dying languages may be revived in the name of linguistic nationalism

15. Which of the following is **not** an example of linguistic nationalism?

    a. You are a Spanish-speaking person in the United States and want your children to learn English, so that they can assimilate more completely into the society around them

    b. A national committee in France declares that certain widely used terms will no longer be allowed to appear in public print because they are not French

    c. You live in Scotland and are so alarmed by the rapid decline in the number of people speaking Gaelic that you start a school in which all subjects are taught in Gaelic

    d. The southern part of India declares itself a separate country called Tamiland (the land of the people who speak Tamil) in defiance of India's declaration of Hindi as the national language; people say they will die in defense of their "mother tongue."

    e. A country previously colonized by the British passes a law requiring everyone to speak the native tongue; English is banned because of its association with colonial domination

16. The influence of a person's class status on what pronunciation he/she uses; a speaker's choice of more complicated vocabulary and grammar when he/she is speaking to a professional audience; the influence of language on culture-all these are the concerns of _____.

    a. descriptive linguistics

    b. historical linguistics

    c. ethnolinguistics

    d. linguistic nationalism

    e. displacement

17. Which of the following statements about the theory of linguistic relativity is **incorrect**?

    a. It was first formulated by Edward Sapir and Benjamin Whorf

    b. It may be briefly explained with the sentence, "Language determines the reality that speakers of the language perceive."

    c. It may be briefly explained with the sentence, "Language reflects reality; it only mirrors what people perceive."

    d. It is expressed in this example: If in a factory a metal drum is labeled "empty" (when in fact it is filled with flammable fumes), people will perceive it as empty and may do things with it that may create a fire hazard (such as storing it near a furnace); but if it is labeled "full" of gaseous fumes, people will perceive it as a fire hazard and treat it more carefully

    e. none of these are incorrect

18. The term _____ is usually used to refer to varying forms of a language that reflect particular regions or social classes and that are similar enough to be mutually intelligible.

    a. dialect

    b. language subgroup

    c. language family

    d. linguistic nationalism

    e. linguistic relativity

19. On April 10, 1984, the _____ became the first community of Native Americans in the United States to affirm the right of its members to regain and maintain fluency in the ancestral language.

    a. Southern Paiute

    b. Northern Paiute

    c. Northern Ute

    d. Isleta Pueblo

    e. Apache

20. The very names for this dialect reflect the diversity of views. Which of the following are **not** terms used to refer to Ebonics.

    a. African American English (AAE)

    b. African American Vernacular (AAVE)

    c. Black English (BE)

    d. African American Dialect (AAD)

    e. they are all terms that refer to Ebonics

21. Which of the following is **not** true of Black English?

    a. It has a short history

    b. It has logical rules of grammar

    c. Its discourse practices cannot be traced

    d. It has an oral literature worthy of respect

    e. "It has a short history" and "Its discourse practices cannot be traced"

22. A specialty within linguistic anthropology that has become almost a separate field of inquiry is _____.

    a. sociolinguistics

    b. historical linguistics

    c. ethnolinguistics

    d. descriptive linguistics

    e. kinesics

23. The theory of linguistic relativity was once known as the _____.

    a. Edward-Benjamin hypothesis

    b. Haviland hypothesis

    c. theory of cultural relativity

    d. theory of linguistic divergence

    e. Sapir-Whorf hypothesis

24. Although we are genetically programmed to speak, what we speak is determined by our _____.

    a. parents

    b. teachers

    c. linguists

    d. culture

    e. genetic make-up

25. The first step in studying any language, once a number of utterances have been collected, is to isolate the _____.

    a. verbs

    b. nouns

    c. phonemes

    d. adjectives

    e. adverbs

26. One of the strengths of modern descriptive linguistics is the _____ of its methods.

    a. subjectivity

    b. clarity

    c. objectivity

    d. simplicity

    e. consistency

27. In North America scratching one's scalp, biting one's lip, or knitting one's brows are ways of conveying doubt. They are also what linguists call _____.

    a. morphology

    b. phonology

    c. sociolinguistic

    d. kinesics

    e. sign language

28. This approach concentrates on the way languages function now, as if they were separate systems, consistent within themselves, without any reference to historical reasons for their development.

    a. descriptive linguistics

    b. glottochronology

    c. diachronic linguistics

    d. historical linguistics

    e. phonology

29. _____ proposed that a language is not simply an encoding process for voicing our ideas and needs but, rather, is a shaping force, which, by providing habitual grooves of expression that predispose people to see the world in a certain way, guides their thinking and behavior.

    a. Benjamin Lee Whorf

    b. Noah Chomsky

    c. Paul Bohannan

    d. Emile Durkheim

    e. Robbins Burling

30. This branch of linguistics involves unraveling a language by recording, describing, and analyzing all of its features.

    a. Social

    b. Descriptive

    c. Historical

    d. Biographical

    e. Phonetical

31. At least _____ percent of our total communication takes place nonverbally.

    a. 25

    b. 75

    c. 15

    d. 40

    e. 60

32. The cross-cultural study of humankind's perception and use of space, came to the fore through the work of anthropologist _____.

    a. Edward Hall.

    b. Benjamin B. Whorf.

    c. Alessandro Duranti.

    d. Gary B. Palmer.

    e. George Urioste.

33. Specialists in this branch of linguistics investigate relationships between earlier and later forms of the same language, older languages for developments in modern ones, and questions of relationships among older language.
    a. Descriptive
    b. Social
    c. Historical
    d. Phonetic
    e. Proxemics

34. When a person has the ability to comprehend two languages, but expresses herself/himself in only one, is known as _____ bilingualism.
    a. negative
    b. positive
    c. true
    d. false
    e. passive

35. It has been suggested that the alphabet was invented about _____ years ago by Semitic-speaking peoples.
    a. 4,000
    b. 2,000
    c. 10,500
    d. 7,500
    e. 3,200

36. It has been nearly 5,000 years since literacy emerged in Egypt and Iraq. Yet, today more than _____ million adults worldwide are illiterate.
    a. 25
    b. 970
    c. 550
    d. 860
    e. 75

True/False Practice Questions

1. Haviland traces linguistics back to the ancient grammarians in China more than three thousand years ago.
   True or False

2. Glottochronology assumes that the rate at which a language's core vocabulary changes is variable and thus cannot be used to give an exact date for when two languages diverged.
   True or False

3. Human culture as we know it could have easily existed without language.
   True or False

4. Though men and women in North American culture typically utilize slightly different vocabularies, the body language they use does not differ much.
   True or False

5. The emphasis on the French language by Quebecois separatists is an example of linguistic nationalism.
   True or False

6. "Ebonics" is a substandard or defective dialect of English.
   True or False

7. The Oakland Public Schools wanted to teach Black English in its schools.
   True or False

8. There was a sense of outrage among some that a stigmatized variety of English would be treated as a valid way of talking in the Oakland Public Schools.
   True or False

9. There is really very little difference between Black English (BE) and Standard English (SE).
   True or False

10. The Oakland school board wrongfully concluded that teachers needed to understand the differences between Standard English and Black English to properly teach children.
    True or False

11. Black English is not just some random form of "broken-down English" intrinsically inferior to Standard English but is a speech variety with its own long history.
    True or False

12. The problem with Black English is that its rules of grammar are illogical.
    True or False

13. Black English has discourse practices traceable to West African languages and a vibrant oral literature worthy of respect.
    True or False

14. In general, Black English has not added much to the vocabulary of American English.
    True or False

15. A major criticism of the Oakland school board's proposal to teach Ebonics is that teachers would be wasting time "teaching" African American Vernacular English when kids should be learning Standard English.
    True or False

16. According to linguistic anthropologist Ron Kephart, the most important work that anthropologists and linguists have to do is to raise public awareness and understanding of what linguistic, cultural and biological differences mean, and most importantly, what they don't mean.
    True or False

17. What the Oakland School Board proposed in regards to teaching Ebonics is no different from what is being done, with considerable success, in several other countries.
    True or False

18. No language uses more than about 100 sounds to communicate.
    True or False

19. Human language is always embedded within a gesture-call system of a type we share with monkeys and apes.
    True or False

20. Cross-cultural research has shown few similarities around the world for such basic facial expressions as smiling, laughing, crying, and variations of anger.
    True or False

21. Like Spanish, English distinguishes between feminine and masculine nouns.
    True or False

22. By applying a logarithmic formula to two related core vocabularies, one can determine how many years two languages have been separated.
    True or False

Practice Matching

Match the term to its definition.

1. _____ bound morpheme
2. _____ phonemes
3. _____ form classes
4. _____ kinesics
5. _____ glottochronology

a. A method of dating divergence within language families.
b. The smallest classes of sound that make a difference in meaning.
c. A sound that occurs in a language only in combination with other sounds, as s in English to signify the plural.
d. Postures, facial expressions, and body motion.
e. The parts of speech that work the same in any sentence.

Practice Short Answer

1. Identify the branches of the science of linguistics.

2. What is a "free morpheme?" Define and provide an example.

3. What accounts for the universality of various cries and facial expressions, as well as for the great difficulty people have in bluffing or especially lying through gesture-calls.

4. Explain why Mandarin Chinese is considered a tonal language and English is not.

5. Among other things, the way a person stands often reveals something about his or her gender. Provide examples to support this observation.

6. Provide an example of a language that uses gendered speech, and explain why is it considered gendered speech?

Practice Essays

1. Would it be accurate to claim language as a distinguishing feature of *H. sapiens*? Why or why not? What evidence exists for the uniqueness or non-uniqueness of human language?

2. How is language linked to gender? Use examples from the text and add some of your own.

3. What was the Northern Ute Language Renewal Project?

4. Of central importance to the development of human culture is language. How might language have started in the first place?

5. What is the theory of linguistic relativity? What do its detractors say about it?

6. Gender language reveals how women and men relate to each other. Exactly what does it reveal about how women and men relate?

7. Perhaps the most powerful force for linguistic change is the domination of one society over another. Provide examples of linguistic change brought about by the domination of one society over another.

8. Discuss Project Chantek and its findings.

9. Although thousands of languages have existed only in spoken form, many have long been documented in one form or writing or another. Discuss the emergence and development of writing systems.

Solutions

Fill-in-the-Blank

1. 6000
2. signal
3. 50
4. 1500s
5. Phonetics
6. phoneme
7. morpheme
8. grammar
9. substitution
10. Paralanguage
11. qualities
12. segregates
13. Kinesics
14. Historical
15. Indo-European
16. nationalism
17. sociolinguistics
18. code switching

Multiple-Choice Practice Questions

1. C
2. B
3. C
4. D
5. A
6. B
7. D
8. E
9. C
10. C
11. E
12. E
13. E
14. B
15. A
16. C
17. C
18. A
19. C
20. D
21. E
22. C
23. E
24. D
25. C
26. C
27. D
28. A
29. A
30. B
31. E
32. A
33. C
34. E
35. A
36. D

True/False Practice Questions

1. F
2. F
3. T
4. F
5. T
6. F
7. F
8. T
9. F
10. F
11. T
12. F
13. T
14. F
15. T
16. T
17. T
18. F
19. T
20. F
21. F
22. T

Practice Matching

1. C
2. B
3. E
4. D
5. A

Chapter 5

Social Identity, Personality, and Gender

Synopsis

Chapter 5 focuses on how culture is transmitted from one generation to the next and explores the cultural contexts in which personalities are formed. It suggests a relativistic understanding of normality and abnormality and looks at recent changes in the field of psychological anthropology.

What You Should Learn from This Chapter

I.   Understand the process and agents of enculturation.

II.   Understand how the behavioral environment functions.

III.   Understand how personality is shaped.

IV.   Understand the concepts of dependence and independence training in child rearing.

V.   Know how group personality is determined.

VI.   Understand the purpose and criticism of national character studies.

VII.   Know how normality and abnormality are defined.

Key Terms and Names

core values

dependence training

enculturation

ethnic psychoses

independence training

intersexuals

Margaret Mead

mental illness

modal personality

naming ceremonies

national character

personality

Ruth Fulton Benedict

self-awareness

transgenders

Exercise

Briefly identify the cultures listed below, and locate them on the world map.

1. Penobscot

2. Arapesh, Mundugamor, Tchambuli

3. Ju/'hoansi

4. Kwakiutl

5. Yanomami

6. Dobu

7. Melemchi

8. Algonkian Indians

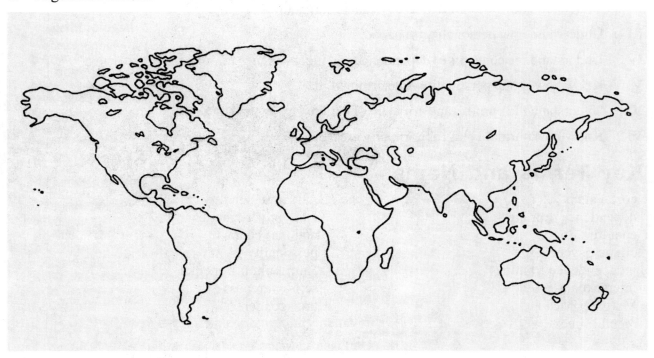

Exersise

Review Questions

1. Who are the agents of enculturation?

2. What are three aspects of self-awareness, according to Haviland?

3. Why might North American children's motor development lag behind that of children from non-Western societies?

4. What are three aspects of the behavioral environment?

5. What does the study of the Penobscot tell us about culture and personality?

6. Describe the situation of the Ju/'hoansi.

7. It was stated that what has seemed to be "normal" in the past, could become "abnormal" in the future. And conversely, it is also true that the abnormal may become the normal. What is meant by these statements?

8. Distinguish between dependence and independence training.

9. What did Margaret Mead's study of adolescent Samoans tell us?

10. Provide an example of modal personality.

11. Explain the basic statistics behind the concept of modal personality.

12. What purpose do the Rorschach and Thematic Appreception Tests serve?

13. What does Francis Hsu suggest are major personality traits of the Chinese?

14. What problems accompany the use of modal personality assessment?

15. What contribution did Ruth Benedict make to the field of culture-and-personality?

16. Why were national character studies undertaken?

17. What was Gorer's toilet-training hypothesis?

18. What are the major objections to national character studies?

19. Provide examples of core values.

20. What is the function of the *two-spirit* in Plains Indians society?

21. How are male and female role identities shaped by the structure of the human family, according to Nancy Chodorow?

22. How is abnormal behavior defined?

23. How are cures effected among the Melemchi of Nepal?

24. What is "windigo?"

Fill-in-the-Blank

1. The Enlightenment thinker John Locke presented the concept of _____ to express the idea that humans are born as "blank slates" and that everything depends on experience.

2. The term _____ refers to the process by which culture is transmitted from one generation to the next.

3. The Penobscot traditionally conceived of the self as divided into two parts, the body and the _____ .

4. Margaret Mead studied three societies in _____ and found out that sex roles were highly variable.

5. Margaret Mead was a founder of the field called _____ .

6. The Ju/'hoansi made a living by _____ in the Kalahari Desert.

7. A concept that attempted to retain the idea of a group personality and yet take into account the diversity of personalities within a group is the concept of _____ .

8. The ink-blot test is properly called the _____ test.

9. The studies developed during World War II to explore the idea that modern nations could be characterized by personality types were called _____ studies.

10. The psychosis exhibited by northern Algonkian Indian groups who recognize the existence of cannibalistic monsters is called _____ .

Multiple-Choice Practice Questions

1. Enculturation is the process of transmitting _____.

   a. society from one generation to the next

   b. social norms from one adult to another

   c. culture from one child to another

   d. culture from one generation to the next

   e. personality from parent to child

2. The agents of enculturation _____.

   a. are persons involved in transmitting culture to the next generation

   b. are at first the members of the family into which the child is born

   c. vary, depending on the structure of the family into which a child is born

   d. include peer groups and schoolteachers

   e. "are persons involved in transmitting culture to the next generation", "are at first the members of the family into which the child is born", "vary, depending on the structure of the family into which a child is born" and "include peer groups and schoolteachers"

3. Which of the following statements about self-awareness is **incorrect**?

   a. Self-awareness occurs earlier in children as a function of the amount of social stimulation they receive

   b. At fifteen weeks of age, the home-reared infant in North America is in contact with its mother for about 20 percent of time

   c. At fifteen weeks of age, infants in the Ju/'hoansi society of South Africa's Kalahari Desert are in close contact with their mothers about 70 percent of the time

   d. American children develop self-awareness earlier than do Ju/'hoansi children

   e. "Self-awareness occurs earlier in children as a function of the amount of social stimulation they receive", "At fifteen weeks of age, the home-reared infant in North America is in contact with its mother for about 20 percent of time", "At fifteen weeks of age, infants in the Ju/'hoansi society of South Africa's Kalahari Desert are in close contact with their mothers about 70 percent of the time" and "American children develop self-awareness earlier than do Ju/'hoansi children"

4. The _____ includes definitions and explanations of objects, spatial orientation, and temporal orientation, as well as culturally defined values, ideals, and standards that provide an individual with a normative orientation.

   a. vital self

   b. *tabula rasa*

   c. behavioral environment

   d. patterns of affect

   e. core values

5. In studying three societies in New Guinea, Margaret Mead found that the role played by men and women were determined primarily by _____.

    a. genes

    b. biology

    c. culture

    d. incest

    e. the food they ate

6. Margaret Mead's groundbreaking work in culture and personality published in 1928 was a deliberate test of a Western psychological hypothesis. What was this hypothesis?

    a. Lowering the drinking age will promote promiscuity

    b. Child-rearing practices have no effect on adult personality

    c. The stress and conflict experienced by American adolescents is a universal phenomenon based on maturing hormones

    d. By changing child-rearing practices, we can change the structure of society

    e. By lowering the driving age, we can promote less stress among adolescents

7. A study of child rearing among the Ju/'hoansi of Africa indicates that _____.

    a. boys and girls are raised in a very similar manner and are both mild-mannered and self-reliant

    b. because girls are out gathering most of the time, they are expected to be more aggressive and self-reliant than boys are

    c. mothers spend the least amount of time with their children, and thus the children identify strongly with their fathers

    d. boys do more work than girls

    e. boys have less responsibility than girls and get to play more of the time

8. Independence training, according to Child and Whitings, is more likely in _____.

    a. small nuclear families

    b. large extended families

    c. small-scale horticultural societies where a man has many wives

    d. a pastoralist family where a woman has many husbands and the extended family has to be always on the move

    e. New York City neighborhoods where large families stay nearby and support each other

9. Dependence training is more likely in _____.

    a. nuclear families

    b. societies whose subsistence is based on pastoralism

    c. a food-foraging society

    d. extended families in societies whose economy is based on subsistence farming

    e. industrial societies

10. The personality typical of a society, as indicated by the central tendency of a defined frequence distribution, is called _____.

    a. core values

    b. nuclear personality

    c. patterns of affect

    d. culture and personality

    e. modal personality

11. Which of the following statements about modal personality is correct?

    a. Although a modal personality may be found for a particular society, a range of personalities may exist in that society

    b. Although the modal personality may be considered "normal" for that society, it may be shared by less than half of the population

    c. Those who study modal personality accept the fact that there may be abnormal individuals in that society

    d. Data on modal personality are usually gathered by the use of psychological tests such as the Rorschach and TAT

    e. "Although a modal personality may be found for a particular society, a range of personalities may exist in that society", "Although the modal personality may be considered "normal" for that society, it may be shared by less than half of the population", "Those who study modal personality accept the fact that there may be abnormal individuals in that society" and "Data on modal personality are usually gathered by the use of psychological tests such as the Rorschach and TAT"

12. Studies of _____ were developed during World War II to explore the idea that basic personality traits were shared by most of the people in modern nations.

    a. modal personality

    b. national character

    c. stereotype

    d. group personality

    e. independence training

13. The term "core values" refers to _____.

    a. those aspects of culture that pertain to the way a culture makes its living

    b. rules that guide family and home life

    c. those values emphasized by a particular culture

    d. common shares in Golden Delicious Corp

    e. the beliefs stressed by a particular political party

14. Among the Plains Indians, a man who wore women's clothes, performed women's work, and married another man _____.

    a. was considered normal

    b. was sought out as a curer, artist, and matchmaker

    c. was assumed to have great spiritual power

    d. might have been homosexual

    e. "was considered normal", "was sought out as a curer, artist, and matchmaker", "was assumed to have great spiritual power" and "might have been homosexual"

15. An ethnic psychosis refers to a _____.

    a. psychotic episode experienced by a person from an exotic culture

    b. progressive disease that strikes anthropologists when they spend more than twelve months in the field

    c. psychosis characterized by symptoms peculiar to a particular group

    d. universal form of mental illness

    e. biologically based disease that resembles schizophrenia

16. Traditional culture and personality studies _____.

    a. were important in undermining ethnocentrism

    b. are criticized today for being impressionistic and difficult to replicate

    c. diversified the study of psychological processes in a cultural context

    d. promoted a relativistic point of view

    e. "were important in undermining ethnocentrism", "are criticized today for being impressionistic and difficult to replicate", "diversified the study of psychological processes in a cultural context" and "promoted a relativistic point of view"

17. According to your textbook, among the Yanomami _____.

    a. all men are fierce and warlike

    b. all men are quiet and retiring

    c. there is a range of personalities

    d. a quiet, retiring Yanomamo would not survive

    e. a fierce, warlike Yanomamo would not survive

18. In _____ infants generally do not sleep with their parents, most often being put in rooms of their own. This is seen as an important step in making them into individuals, "owners" of themselves and their capacities, rather than part of some social whole.

    a. the Ituri rain forest

    b. China

    c. the United States

    d. Mexico

    e. the Kalahari Desert

19. As _____ pioneering studies suggested, whatever biological differences may exist between men and women, they are extremely malleable.

    a. Ruth Benedict's

    b. Karen Sacks's

    c. Deborah Tannen's

    d. Margaret Mead's

    e. Laura Nader's

20. One of the "founding mothers" of anthropology is _____.

    a. Nancy Scheper-Hughes

    b. Catherine Bateson

    c. Mary Douglas

    d. Margaret Mead

    e. Emily Schultz

21. Today in Native American societies the preferred term to describe an individual who falls between the categories of "man" and "woman" is known as _____.

    a. berdache

    b. gay

    c. passive homosexual

    d. two-spirit

    e. effeminate

22. We should not be surprised to find that explanations of the universe are never entirely objective in nature, but are _____.

    a. culturally constructed

    b. figments of one's imagination

    c. scientifically constructed

    d. evolved historically

    e. simply absurd

23. Usually regarded as dreaded liabilities, anthropologist _____ suggests that, in North America, aspects of manic-depression and Attention Deficit Hyperactivity Disorder (ADHD) are coming to be seen as assets in the quest for success.

    a. Jennifer Thompson

    b. Vicki Cassman

    c. Emily Martin

    d. Martha Knack

    e. William Jankowiak

24. All societies must somehow ensure that their culture is adequately transmitted from one generation to the next. This transmission process is known as _____.

    a. acculturation

    b. assimilation

    c. enculturation

    d. absorption

    e. integration

25. When first encountered by Europeans, the _____ conceived of each individual as being made of two parts-the body and a personal spirit.

    a. Apache

    b. Onondaga

    c. Penobscot

    d. Menominee

    e. Iroquois

26. The _____ personality is the personality typical of a society as indicated by the central tendency of a defined frequency distribution.

    a. normal

    b. average

    c. standard

    d. mean

    e. modal

27. Data on modal personality are best gathered with psychological tests administered to a sample of the population in question. Those most often used would include which of the following?

    a. SAT

    b. Rorschach, or inkblot test

    c. DAP (Draw a Person Test)

    d. TAT (thematic Apperception Test)

    e. Rorschach, or inkblot test and TAT (thematic Apperception Test)

28. Among the _____, a widely held belief is that spirits are active in the world and that they influence human behavior.

    a. Germans

    b. French

    c. Argentinians

    d. Puerto Ricans

    e. Spanish

29. _____ is a fear reaction often occurring in middle-aged Malay women of low intelligence who are subservient and self-effacing.

    a. Koro

    b. Saka

    c. Windigo

    d. Pibloktoq

    e. Latah

30. Among the _____, naming a child was traditionally the right of the clan mother, the senior-ranking female elder in a cluster of related families.

    a. Icelanders

    b. Aymara Indians

    c. Hopi

    d. Netsilik Inuit

    e. Iroquois

31. _____ orientation includes standards that indicate what ranges of behavior are acceptable for males and females in a particular society.

    a. Spatial

    b. Temporal

    c. Normative

    d. Objective

    e. Gender

True/False Practice Questions

1. What is considered "normal" in a society is defined by culture.
   True or False

2. Anthropologists believe that all mental illness is learned rather than biologically based.
   True or False

3. Both hunting and gathering societies and industrial societies promote independence training in their mobile nuclear families.
   True or False

4. Margaret Mead believed that male and female roles were by and large defined by the biological attributes of the sexes.
   True or False

5. National character studies developed during World War II to explore the idea that basic personality traits were shared by most of the people in modern nations.
   True or False

6. The primary contribution of Whiting and Child to the field of psychological anthropology was their in-depth study of the Ju/'hoansi.
   True or False

7. The Yanomami of Brazil are known for their "fierceness," yet there is a range of personality types even there.
   True or False

8. The Native American view sees intersexed individuals in a very positive and affirming light.
   True or False

9. The Euro-American view of intersexed individuals is similar to the Native American view.
   True or False

10. The extent to which Native Americans see spirituality is reflected in their belief that all things have spirit.
    True or False

11. From the Native American perspective the spirit of a human is superior to the spirit of any other thing.
    True or False

12. To Native Americans the function of religion is not to try to condemn or to change what exists, but to accept the realities of the world and to appreciate their contributions.
    True or False

13. Native American believe everything that exists has a purpose.
    True or False

14. An intersexed child is derided and viewed as a "freak of nature" in traditional Native American culture.
    True or False

15. What was abnormal in the past may become normal.
    True or False

16. Today, for a man to assume a feminine identity is not regarded as abnormal by European-Americans; in fact, such individuals are regarded as special in that they bridge the gap between the purely feminine and purely masculine.
    True or False

17. In food-foraging societies child-rearing practices combine elements of both dependence and independence training.
    True or False

18. As hard as they have tried, anthropologists have never found a quiet and retiring Yanomami man.
    True or False

19. What defines normal behavior in any culture is determined by the culture itself, and what may be acceptable, or even admirable, in one may not be in another.
    True or False

20. Breast-feeding tends to be relatively long-lived in the industrialized world, due to workplace conditions which facilitate it.
    True or False

21. It has become clear that each culture provides different opportunities and has different expectations for ideal or acceptable male-female behavior.
    True or False

22. Clearly, the biological capacity for what we think of as humanhood, which entails culture, must be nurtured to be realized.
    True or False

Short Answer Practice Questions

1. Describe the Icelander's ancient naming custom.

2. What do the Aymara of highland Bolivia think about the naming of a child.

3. Discuss the naming process in Hopi culture.

4. Describe the Netsilik Inuit naming process.

5. Common sense suggests that personalities appropriate for one culture may be less appropriate for others. Provide examples that would support this statement.

Practice Essays

1. It was stated that what has seemed to be "normal" in the past, could become "abnormal" in the future. And conversely, it is also true that the abnormal may become the normal. What is meant by these statements? Provide examples.

2. What was the impact of Freudian psychoanalysis on the development of psychological anthropology? How have culture-and-personality specialists responded to the Freudian paradigm?

3. What is the traditional Penobscot concept of self? What did it have to do with their behavioral environment?

4. The author of the original study The Blessed Curse mentioned, "from a very early age I was presented with two different and conflicting views of myself." What did the author mean by this? Explain.

5. Explain why the Native American and Euro-American views on intersexuality are so diametrically opposed.

6. Discuss the importance of child-rearing practices for the development of gender related personality characteristics. Provide examples.

7. Explain why child rearing practices in the United States creates problems of gender identity for both sexes, although a different sort for each sex.

8. How does a culture itself induce certain kinds of psychological conflicts that have important consequences for the entire society?

9. The original study is entitled "The Blessed Curse: A Foot in Both Worlds." What is the explanation for this rather unusual title?

10. Using examples, explain the importance of a child-rearing practices in the development of gender-related personality characteristics.

11. How does a society's economy help structure the way a child is brought up and how does this, influence the development of the adult personality?

12. There are people who do not fit neatly into a binary gender standard. Identify those people and explain why they don't fit neatly into a binary gender standard.

13. Describe the range of inherited and artificially imposed sexual features that human cultures have dealt with in the course of thousands of years.

Solutions

Fill-in-the-Blank

1. tabula rasa
2. enculturation
3. personal spirit
4. New Guinea
5. Culture and Personality
6. food foraging
7. modal personality
8. Rorschach
9. national character
10. windigo

Multiple-Choice Practice Questions

1. D
2. E
3. D
4. C
5. C
6. C
7. A
8. A
9. D
10. E
11. E
12. B
13. C
14. E
15. C
16. E
17. C
18. C
19. D
20. D
21. D
22. A
23. C
24. C
25. C
26. E
27. E
28. D
29. E
30. E
31. C

True/False Practice Questions

1. T
2. F
3. T
4. F
5. T
6. F
7. T
8. T
9. F
10. T
11. F
12. T
13. T
14. F
15. T
16. F
17. T
18. F
19. T
20. F
21. T
22. T

Chapter 6

Patterns of Subsistence

Synopsis

In Chapter 6 the text examines the impact that various modes of subsistence have on cultures. Food foraging is described in detail, and the variations in food production systems are discussed.

What You Should Learn from This Chapter

I. Understand the role of adaptation in cultural survival:
   A. unit of adaptation
   B. evolutionary adaptation
   C. culture areas
   D. culture core

II. Understand the food-foraging way of life:
   A. subsistence and sex roles
   B. food sharing
   C. cultural adaptations and material technology
   D. egalitarian society

III. Understand food-producing society:
   A. Horticulturalist
   B. Pastoralist
   C. intensive agriculture and preindustrial cities

Key Terms and Names

adaptation
carrying capacity
convergent evolution
cultural ecology
culture area
culture core
culture type
density of social relations
ecosystem

ethnoscientists
horticulture
Julian Steward
Neolithic Revolution
parallel evolution
pastoralist
preindustrial cities
swidden
transhumance

Exercises

1. Complete the chart below, filling in examples of each type of subsistence and noting its general characteristics. You can use this to study from later.

PATTERNS OF SUBSISTENCE		
Type	Example	Characteristics
Foraging		
Pastoralism		
Horticlture		
Intensive Agriculture		

2. Briefly identify the cultures listed below, and locate them on the world map.

A. Tsembaga

B. Comanche

C. Shoshone and Paiute

D. Hadza

E. Mekranoti

F. Gurumba

G. Bakhtiari

H. Innu

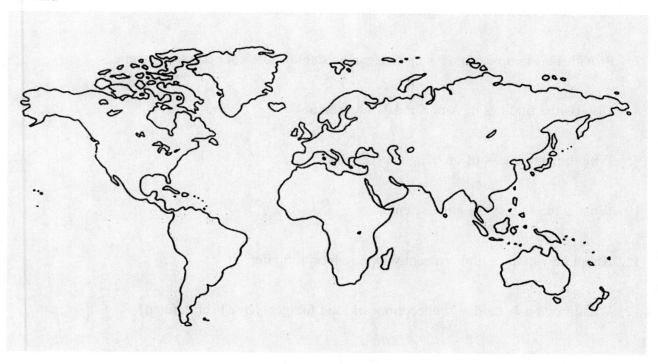

Exercise

Review Questions

1. What purpose does adaptation serve?

2. Describe the relationship the Tsembaga have with the environment.

3. Explain what is meant by a unit of adaptation.

4. What are human ecologists concerned with?

5. Describe Comanche adaptation to the plains environment.

6. Distinguish between convergent and parallel evolution.

7. Provide an example of how a culture can be stable while not necessarily static.

8. Discuss the findings of Ann Kendall's research?

9. Why did native groups on the plains not farm?

10. What is the role of the ethnoscientist?

11. About how many people currently live by food foraging?

12. What previously held misconceptions of food foragers have been refuted?

13. What are the main social characteristics of food foragers?

14. What are the size-limiting factors in a foraging group?

15. What purpose does population redistribution serve for the Ju/'hoansi?

16. What impact does biological sex have on the division of labor?

17. How is the behavior of food-foraging groups reflected in their material culture?

18. Why are food foragers generally egalitarian?

19. Can we make any generalizations about the status of women in foraging societies?

20. How is territory conceptualized in foraging societies?

21. Define the concerns of Julian Steward's study of cultural ecology.

22. Distinguish between horticulturalists and intensive agriculturalists.

23. What are the basic features of pastoralist society?

24. Define "adaptation" and "ecosystem" and illustrate the relevance of these concepts with the example of pig sacrifices among the Tsembaga.

25. Why has slash-and-burn (swidden) come to be viewed negatively by many people today?

26. Describe the subsistence practices of the Mekranoti.

27. What did anthropologist Ann Kendall learn from the past mistakes of indigenous peoples of the Patacacha Valley in the Andes Mountains of southern Peru?

Fill-in-the-Blank

1. _____ is the process by which organisms modify and adjust to their environment and thereby survive more effectively.

2. The main animal raised by the Gururumba are _____ .

3. When the Comanche migrated to the Great Plains, they found a new food source, the _____ .

4. When several societies with different cultural backgrounds move into a new environment and develop similar adaptations, they represent the cultural equivalent of _____ evolution.

5. When several societies with very similar cultural backgrounds develop along similar lines, they represent the process of _____ evolution.

6. A geographic region in which a number of different societies follow a similar pattern of life is called a culture _____ .

7. The various societies of the Great Plains had common religious rituals, such as _____ .

8. The subfield within anthropology that studies the interaction of specific cultures with their environments is called _____ .

9. The anthropologist who pioneered this subfield was _____ .

10. _____ try to understand folk ideologies and how they help a group survive.

11. Humans lived using food foraging until about _____ years ago, when domestication of animals and plants began.

12. The Ju/'hoansi of the Kalahari Desert have been called "the original _____ society" because they work so few hours a week.

13. The number of people who can be supported by a certain technology is the _____ of the environment.

14. About _____ percent of the diet of most food foragers is gathered by women.

15. Increased food sharing appears to be related to a shift in food habits involving increased eating of _____ around two and a half million years ago.

16. Another name for slash-and-burn is _____ farming.

17. The Bakhtiari of the Zagros Mountains are _____ who migrate seasonally from one location to another.

18. City life is based on a subsistence pattern of _____ .

19. The main city of the Aztecs was _____ .

20. The anthropologist who conducted her research in the Andes Mountains of southern Peru was _____ .

Multiple-Choice Practice Questions

1. Adaptation refers to the _____.
    a. process by which organisms modify and adjust to their environment and thereby survive more effectively
    b. ability of one population to destroy another
    c. borrowing of cultural material from another society
    d. process by which living systems change from birth to death
    e. effect of child-rearing practices on basic personality structure

2. Before the arrival of horses and guns, the Comanche were food foragers in southern Idaho. Their skill as hunters was put to good use as they used these new tools to hunt buffalo on the Great Plains. The term used to refer to existing customs that by chance have potential for a new cultural adaptation is _____.

   a. convergent evolution

   b. divergent evolutions

   c. ecosystem

   d. parallel evolution

   e. preadaptations

3. The Comanche and the Cheyenne were quite different culturally until they moved out onto the Great Plains and made use of the horse to hunt buffalo and raid settled peoples. They then became more similar in cultural adaptations, a process called _____.

   a. preadaptation

   b. development of a culture area

   c. convergent evolution

   d. parallel evolution

   e. an ecosystem

4. Native American food foragers established a way of life in New England and southern Quebec that lasted about five thousand years. This is indicative of _____.

   a. stagnation

   b. failure to progress

   c. genetic inferiority

   d. lack of innovation

   e. effective cultural adaptation

5. A culture type is defined by _____.

   a. the geographic area in which a people live

   b. the kind of technology that a group has to exploit a particular environment

   c. contacts with other cultures

   d. sharing the same values

   e. sharing the same language

6. A taboo against eating certain foods, the belief that only a chief has strong enough magic to plant apple trees and dispense them to his fellow villagers, and the number of hours a people work each day are examples of what could be considered part of a society's _____.

   a. structural base

   b. foundation

   c. infrastructure

   d. culture core

   e. none of these

7. Which of the following research topics might be of interest to an ethnoscientist?

    a. How the allele responsible for sickle-cell anemia increases or decreases in certain cultural environments, such a horticultural vs. hunting-gathering.

    b. Similarities and differences in the farming patterns of Southwest Asia and Mesoamerica

    c. The ways in which a group classifies and explains the world; for example, the Tsembaga avoid low-lying, marshy areas filled with mosquitoes that carry malaria because they believe that such areas are inhabited by red spirits who punish trespassers

    d. Reconstruction and comparison of archaeological sites in similar geographic regions

    e. "How the allele responsible for sickle-cell anemia increases or decreases in certain cultural environments, such a horticultural vs. hunting-gathering", "Similarities and differences in the farming patterns of Southwest Asia and Mesoamerica", "The ways in which a group classifies and explains the world; for example, the Tsembaga avoid low-lying, marshy areas filled with mosquitoes that carry malaria because they believe that such areas are inhabited by red spirits who punish trespassers" and "Reconstruction and comparison of archaeological sites in similar geographic regions"

8. Some anthropologists refer to food foragers as "the original affluent society" because _____.

    a. they manage to accumulate a lot of wealth

    b. they occupy the most attractive environments with abundant food supply

    c. they live in marginal areas and are very poor

    d. they earn a good wage for all hours of work they put in each week

    e. they work only twelve to nineteen hours a week for a comfortable, healthy life

9. The groups referred to as food foragers must live where there are naturally available food sources; thus they _____.

    a. remain in permanent settlements

    b. move about once every ten years

    c. move frequently

    d. adopt farming whenever they can

    e. prefer to live in cities

10. The number and intensity of interactions among the members of a residential unit is called _____.

    a. density of social relations

    b. social interactionism

    c. cultural ecology

    d. carrying capacity

    e. convergent evolution

11. Which of the following is **not** one of the three elements of human social organization that developed with hunting?
    a. sexual division of labor
    b. aggressive behavior
    c. food sharing
    d. the camp site
    e. "sexual division of labor", "aggressive behavior", "food sharing" and "the camp site"

12. In a food-foraging society, how do people store food for the future?
    a. They keep a surplus in stone cairns
    b. They keep extra plants in large, circular yam houses
    c. They hide meat in each individual family residence
    d. They rely on the generosity of others to share food
    e. They keep dried food in a common storage shed

13. To say that food-foraging societies are egalitarian means that _____.
    a. there are no status differences
    b. the only status differences are age and sex
    c. everyone is equal except women
    d. men are usually subordinate to women
    e. children are the center of community life

14. Someone who uses irrigation, fertilizers, and the plow to produce food on large plots of land is known as a/an _____.
    a. horticulturalists
    b. intensive agriculturalist
    c. pastoralists
    d. hunter-gatherer
    e. industrialist

15. _____ are food producers who specialize in animal husbandry and who consider their way of life to be ideal and central to defining their identities.
    a. Food foragers
    b. Horticulturalists
    c. Intensive agriculturalists
    d. Pastoralists
    e. Industrialists

16. Aztec society in the sixteenth century _____.
    a. was a stratified society based on achievement and education.
    b. was an urbanized society in which kinship played no role in determining status
    c. was an industrial city-state
    d. was invincible to Cortes' attack
    e. none of these

17. Which of the following statements about preindustrial cities is **incorrect**?

    a. Preindustrial cities have existed in some parts of the world for thousands of years

    b. Preindustrial cities represent a stage of development in the progression of human culture toward industrial cities

    c. Tenochtitlan, the capital of the Aztec empire, is a good example of a preindustrial city

    d. Preindustrial cities have a diversified economy

    e. Preindustrial cities are highly stratified

18. This North American developed an approach that he called cultural ecology, that is, the interaction between specific cultures with their environments.

    a. Ann Kendall

    b. Leslie White

    c. Fred Plog

    d. Julian Steward

    e. Barbara Myerhoff

19. After three years of tending their gardens the Mekranoti are left with only _____.

    a. manioc

    b. sweet potatoes

    c. pineapple

    d. tobacco

    e. bananas

20. A society's cultural beliefs, no matter how irrelevant they may seem to outsiders, are anything but irrelevant if one is to understand another society's _____ practices.

    a. marketing

    b. voting

    c. business

    d. trading

    e. subsistence

21. How food-foraging peoples regulate population size relates to which of the following things?

    a. How much body fat they accumulate

    b. The accumulation of material goods

    c. Abortion practices

    d. How they care for their children

    e. "How much body fat they accumulate" and "How they care for their children"

22. Haviland points out in his textbook *Cultural Anthropology*, that _____ is an effective way of living-far more so than ranching.

    a.   food-foraging

    b.   pastoralism

    c.   slash and burn agriculture

    d.   hunting and gathering

    e.   farming

23. The _____ process establishes a moving balance between the needs of a population and the potential of its environment.

    a.   adaptation

    b.   accommodation

    c.   integration

    d.   evolution

    e.   adjustment

24. The kind of development where similar cultural adaptations to similar environmental conditions by peoples whose ancestral cultures were quite different is called _____.

    a.   parallel evolution

    b.   complementary evolution

    c.   concurrent evolution

    d.   affinal evolution

    e.   convergent evolution

25. _____ is the study of the interaction of specific human cultures with their environments.

    a.   Ecological interaction

    b.   Symbolic interaction

    c.   Scientific ecology

    d.   Social ecology

    e.   Cultural ecology

26. The number of people the available resources can support at a given technological level is known as the _____.

    a.   density of social relations

    b.   equilibrium point

    c.   carrying capacity

    d.   point of diminishing capacity

    e.   balanced position

27. Food foragers like the _____ have a division of labor in which women gather and prepare "bush" food, but hunting is usually done by men.

    a. Gros Ventre

    b. Crow

    c. Ju/'hoansi

    d. Mandingo

    e. Tutsi

28. Although we tend to think of people as either food foragers or food producers, there are numerous examples of people like the _____, who rely on a mix of wild and domesticated resources.

    a. Ju/'hoansi

    b. Comanche

    c. Abenaki

    d. Pequot

    e. Papago

29. Aztec agricultural success provided for which of the following?

    a. a highly mobile population

    b. an increasingly large population

    c. the diversification of labor

    d. a more egalitarian society

    e. "an increasingly large population" and "the diversification of labor"

30. Intensive agriculture, a more complex activity than swidden farming, requires which of the following?

    a. irrigation

    b. fertilizers

    c. draft animals

    d. a high level of mobility

    e. "irrigation", "fertilizers" and "draft animals"

31. A people's _____ adaptation consists of a complex of ideas, activities, and technologies that enable them to survive and even thrive.

    a. social

    b. cultural

    c. economic

    d. political

    e. religious

32. Which of the following Native American groups fell within the Great Plains culture area?
    a. Iroquois
    b. Cheyenne
    c. Apache
    d. Comanche
    e. B and D

33. Muslims and Jews have a food taboo against the consumption of _____.
    a. horses.
    b. cattle.
    c. pigs.

D. dogs.
E. cats.

1. American anthropologist _____ referred to food foragers as the "original affluent society."
    a. Franz Boas
    b. Margaret Mead
    c. Ruth Benedict
    d. Marshall Sahlins
    e. A.R. Radcliffe-Brown

2. Because the transition from food foraging to food production brought about radical transformations in every aspect of the cultural systems involved in the move, archaeologist _____ introduced the term "Neolithic Revolution."
    a. Marshall Sahlines
    b. Gordon Childe
    c. Alan Simmons
    d. Franz Boas
    e. J.H. Steward

True/False Practice Questions

1. According to the Original Study, the Mekranoti had to work hard to get enough produce from their gardens.
   True or False

2. The Mbuti live in the Ituri rain forest in the Republic of the Congo.
   True or False

3. The Bakhtiari are pastoralist nomads who drive their herds throughout the Iran-Iraq border area.
   True or False

4. Many Bakhtiari are well-educated, having attended university at home or aboard.
   True or False

5. The spread of malaria was historically linked to the development of slash-and-burn horticulture.
   True or False

6. In the world today about 3 million people live by food foraging.
    True or False

7. People started shifting to food-producing ways of life about ten thousand years ago.
    True or False

8. The average work week of the Ju/'hoansi is about fifty hours.
    True or False

9. An anthropologist would probably find it difficult to define what "progress" is.
    True or False

10. The Mekranoti style of slash-and-burn farming did not grow well because animals and insects were constantly invading their gardens.
    True or False

11. Due to their reliance of slash-and-burn farming the Mekranoti need to work very hard to survive.
    True or False

12. The Mekranoti constantly weed their gardens to keep the forest from invading.
    True or False

13. Slash-and-burn agriculture, especially in the humid tropics, may be one of the best gardening techniques possible.
    True or False

14. Anthropologists were the last to note the possibly disastrous consequences of U.S.-style agriculture in the tropics.
    True or False

15. According agriculturalists, open-field agriculture is less of a problem than slash-and-burn agriculture.
    True or False

16. The high fertility of Mekranoti garden plots comes from the soil, not from the trees that are burned there.
    True or False

17. Because of foraging animals and destructive insects, the Mekranoti could not depend on harvesting whatever they planted.
    True or False

18. The Mekranoti, it was found, don't have to work very hard to survive.
    True or False

19. Among food-foraging peoples teenage pregnancies are rampant.
    True or False

20. Food foraging would certainly not be found in a rich industrial nation such as the United States.
    True or False

21. Among food foragers today, the work of women is no less arduous than that of men.
    True or False

22. There are no sources of status differences among food foragers.
    True or False

23. Today we know that, especially in the humid tropics, slash-and-burn agriculture may be one of the best gardening techniques possible.
    True or False

24. It can be safely said that "preindustrial" cities are very uncommon in today's world.
    True or False

25. All innovations turn out to be positive in the long run, eventually improving conditions for every member of a society.
    True or False

26. Everybody benefits from changes, even if they are forced upon them.
    True or False

27. Notwithstanding the multiple changes that have occurred over the course of many thousands of years, the original division of labor has been eliminated from every culture.
    True or False

28. Today, all the fastest growing cities are in the highly industrialized countries of western Europe.
    True or False

Practice Matching

1.	_____ Tsembaga		a.	They live in Labrador.
2.	_____ Bakhtiari		b.	West Asian pastoralists.
3.	_____ Comanche		c.	Horse people of the Great Plains.
4.	_____ Mbuti		d.	Pig sacrificers of New Guinea.
5.	_____ Innu		e.	Food foragers of the Ituri rain forest.

Practice Short Answer Questions

1. Explain why the development of farming in Southwest Asia and Mesoamerica considered a case of parallel evolution.

2. Explain why anthropologist Marshall Sahlins referred to food foragers as the "original affluent society."

Practice Essays

1. How does Ju/'hoansi social organization relate to the subsistence pattern of hunting and collecting? How is Ju/'hoansi society likely to change as the foraging way of life erodes?

2. Think about your neighborhood. Could it be described as a kind of cultural area, i.e., a geographic region in which a number of different societies follow similar patterns of life? What criteria would be important for defining it that way?

3. The Mekranoti Kayapo employ what has come to be known as slash-and-burn agriculture. Describe the benefits of this style of farming in the tropics. What would be the consequences of a U.S.-style of agriculture in the tropics?

4. As mentioned in your textbook, just as we have much to learn from the successes of indigenous peoples, so can we learn from their mistakes, and the ways they cope with their mistakes. Anthropologist Ann Kendall is doing just this in southern Peru. What did her research discover and what is she doing to rectify the results of the past mistakes of indigenous peoples in the Patacacha Valley in the Andes Mountains?

5. Explain how the anthropologist was able to calculate the productivity of Mekranoti gardens.

6. It is said that "environments do not determine culture but do set certain potentials and limitations." Provide examples to support this statement.

7. What impact has intensive agriculture had on human society?

8. Discuss how the Great Plains became an indigenous culture area.

9. Describe the negative stereotype of food foragers. How did it come about and why is it ill-founded?

Solutions

Fill-in-the-Blank

1. Adaptation
2. pigs
3. buffalo
4. convergent
5. parallel
6. area
7. Ghost Dance
8. cultural ecology
9. Julian H. Steward
10. Ethnoscientists
11. 10,000
12. affluent
13. carrying capacity
14. 60-70
15. meat
16. swidden
17. Pastoral nomads
18. intensive agriculture
19. Tenochtitlan
20. Ann Kendall

Multiple-Choice Practice Questions

1. A
2. E
3. C
4. E
5. B
6. D
7. C
8. E
9. C
10. A
11. B
12. D
13. B
14. B
15. D
16. E
17. B
18. D
19. E
20. E
21. E
22. B
23. A
24. E
25. E
26. C
27. C
28. C
29. E
30. E
31. B
32. E
33. C

Multiple-Choice Practice Questions

34. D
35. B

True/False Practice Questions

1. F
2. T
3. T
4. T
5. T
6. F
7. T
8. F
9. T
10. F
11. F
12. F
13. T
14. F
15. F
16. F
17. F
18. T
19. F
20. F
21. T
22. F
23. T
24. F
25. F
26. F
27. F
28. F

Practice Matching

1. D
2. B
3. C
4. E
5. A

Chapter 7

Economic Systems

Synopsis

Chapter 7 discusses the attempt to apply economic theory to non-Western cultures and summarizes the concepts anthropologists have developed to compare the organization of productive resources across cultures. Three major ways of distributing goods and services are described. The relevance of anthropological understanding to international business is also considered.

What You Should Learn from This Chapter

I. Understand how anthropologists use theory to study economic systems.

II. Know the patterns of labor in nonindustrial societies:
    A. sexual division of labor
    B. division of labor by age
    C. cooperation
    D. craft specialization
    E. control of land
    F. technology

III. Understand the methods of distribution and exchange in nonindustrial societies:
    A. reciprocity
    B. redistribution
    C. market exchange

Key Terms and Names

balanced reciprocity
Big Man
conspicuous consumption
economic system
generalized reciprocity
informal economy
Kula ring
leveling mechanism
market exchange

money
negative reciprocity
potlatch
prestige economy
reciprocity
redistribution
silent trade
technology

Exercises

1. When Bronislaw Malinowski studied the Kula ring of the Trobriand Islanders in his classic *Argonauts of the Western Pacific*, he also described other methods of distributing goods in that society as well. Consider each of the following examples of Trobriand exchanges given by

Malinowski, and identify whether they can be characterized as forms of reciprocity, redistribution, or market exchange. Then note the elements of each of these forms of exchange in modern North American society as well.

A. Wasi: permanent partnerships inland yam-producers inherit with fishermen. When a fisherman brings in a good catch, he takes some fish to his inland partner and gives them as a gift; when the farmer brings in his yam harvest, he takes some to the fisherman as a gift. Neither has any choice about changing partners, neither can bargain for more products, and there is no stated expectation of a return.

B. *Urigubu*: the yam gift that a man gives to his sister's husband every year; it is part of a person's kinship obligations.

C. *Kula*: the exchange between contractual partners of ceremonial/prestige/treasure items.

D. *Pokala*: tribute to a higher-status person, usually a chief.

E. *Sagali*: giveaway feast by a high-status person, usually a chief.

F. *Gim walli*: the moneyless exchange of mundane goods (barter) that occurs after the Kula gift-giving; this exchange occurs between anyone (no contractual partners), and the value seems to be established according to supply and demand and done with a desire to gain the greatest profit.

2. Briefly identify the following cultures, and indicate their locations on the map.
A. Enga
B. Inca
C. Afar
D. Tiv
E. Kota, Toda, Bagada, Kurumba

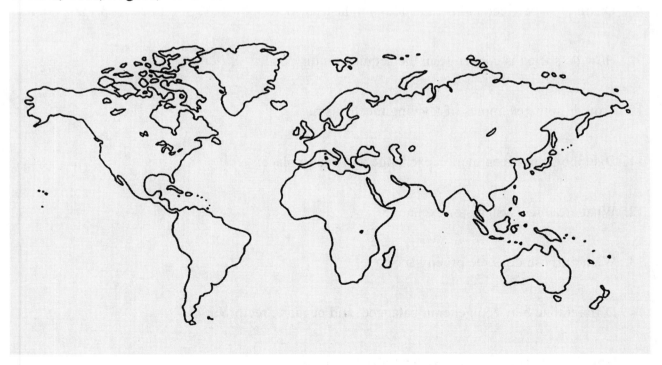

Exercise

Review Questions

1. Why might it be misleading to apply contemporary economic theories to preindustrial non-Western societies?

2. Explain the importance of yam production among the Trobrianders.

3. Provide examples that refute the notion of a biological division of labor.

4. Compare and contrast the three general patterns of the sexual division of labor.

5. What are the benefits of the division of labor?

6. How is land controlled in most preindustrial societies?

7. Differentiate between the use of tools in foraging, horticultural, and agricultural communities.

8. Distinguish between industrial and nonindustrial societies with regard to craft specialization.

9. How do societies cooperate in the acquisition of food?

10. Provide some examples of leveling mechanisms.

11. Distinguish between market exchange and marketplace.

12. What are three systems of exchange?

13. What purpose does reciprocity serve?

14. Differentiate between general, balanced, and negative reciprocity.

15. How is trade between groups generally conducted?

16. As discussed in your textbook, describe the relationships between the Kota, Toda, Badaga, and Kurumba of India.

17. What functions does the Kula ring serve?

18. Compare "money" among the Aztec and the Tiv.

19. Why is redistribution generally undertaken?

20. Describe the "informal economy" of North America.

21. How is conspicuous consumption used?

22. Discuss the relevance of anthropology to international business.

23. What are the drawbacks of ethnocentric interpretations of other societies' economic systems?

24. Discuss the role that culture plays in defining the "wants and needs" of a people.

Fill-in-the-Blank

1. All societies have rules pertaining to three productive resources: _____ , _____ , and _____ .

2. Division of labor by sex varies from very flexible to very rigid. Among foragers like the _____ , either sex may do the work of the other without loss of face.

3. Rigid division of labor by sex typically occurs with two patterns of subsistence: _____ and _____ .

4. In most societies the basic unit in which cooperation takes place is the _____ .

5. Among horticulturalists, tools that are typically used are the _____ , _____ , and _____ .

6. A _____ works to spread wealth around so that no one accumulates substantially more wealth than anyone else.

7. The economist _____ developed the threefold classification system of reciprocity, redistribution, and market exchange.

8. Types of reciprocity are _____ , _____ , and _____ .

9. The taxation systems of Canada and the United States are examples of _____ .

10. In some societies the surplus is used as a display for purposes of prestige. Thorsten Veblen called this _____ .

11. Among the Enga of Papua New Guinea, the group that pools its wealth is the _____ .

12. The Kota, Toda, Badaga, and Kurumba are interrelated societies in _____ .

Multiple-Choice Practice Questions

1. When a man works hard in his horticultural garden in the Trobriand Islands to produce yams, he does this to satisfy which of the following demands?

    a. to have food for his household to eat

    b. to gain prestige by giving yams away to his sisters' husbands

    c. to prove to his wife that he can work as hard as she can

    d. to give the yams to his wife so that she can trade them for goods that they don't produce themselves

    e. to trade for fish

2. The productive resources used by all societies to produce goods and services include _____.

    a. raw materials

    b. labor

    c. technology

    d. bureaucrats

    e. raw materials, labor and technology

3. American society's traditional sexual division of labor falls into which pattern?

    a. flexible

    b. rigid segregation

    c. segregation with equality

    d. integrated

    e. cooperative

4. Among the Ju/'hoansi _____.

    a. children are expected to contribute to subsistence from the time they are seven or eight.

    b. elderly people past the age of sixty are expected to contribute hunted or gathered food to the group.

    c. elderly people are a valuable source of knowledge and wisdom about hunting and gathering.

    d. elderly people are taken care of grudgingly because after the age of sixty they contribute nothing to the group.

    e. children are expected to set up their own separate households by the time they are twelve.

5. In many nonindustrial societies,

    a. people prefer to have fun rather than to work.

    b. cooperative work is usually done with a festive, sociable air.

    c. cooperative work is always done in the household.

    d. cooperative work groups are organized primarily for profit.

    e. solitary work is preferred to cooperative work

6. Among food foragers such as the Ju/'hoansi, _____

    a. land is defined as a territory with usable resources and flexible boundaries that belongs to a band that has occupied it for a long time

    b. land is thought of as belonging to those who have bought it

    c. land is considered private property, and access to the land can be denied

    d. land has clear-cut boundaries marked by survey posts

    e. land is controlled by a corporation of strangers

7. In nonindustrial societies, when a tool is complex and difficult to make it is usually considered to be owned by _____.

    a. the whole village in which it is used

    b. a single individual

    c. the state

    d. all those who touch it

    e. all relatives

8. Leveling mechanisms _____.

    a. are more common in hunter-gatherer societies than in agricultural communities.

    b. result in one family becoming wealthier than others

    c. are found in communities where property must not be allowed to threaten an egalitarian social order

    d. are more common in industrial societies than in agricultural societies

    e. no longer exist

9. The mode of distribution called reciprocity refers to the exchange of goods and services _____.

    a. of unequal value

    b. between persons in hierarchical relationships

    c. for the purpose of maintaining social relationships and gaining prestige

    d. to make a profit

    e. to embarrass the person who gave the least

10. A Navaho gives ten of his sheep that he knows are infected with disease to a Hopi in exchange for a jeep. This is an example of _____.
    a. generalized reciprocity
    b. balanced reciprocity
    c. negative reciprocity
    d. silent trade
    e. redistribution

11. The Kula ring _____.
    a. is a marriage ring made of shells
    b. is found among the Ju/'hoansi
    c. is found among the Andaman Islanders
    d. is a circular trade route along which various goods flow
    e. is a form of silent trade

12. The American system of paying income taxes every April is an example of _____.
    a. generalized reciprocity
    b. balanced reciprocity
    c. negative reciprocity
    d. redistribution
    e. market exchange

13. The display of wealth for social prestige is called _____.
    a. a leveling mechanism
    b. conspicuous consumption
    c. redistribution
    d. balanced reciprocity
    e. barter

14. Formal market exchange is usually associated with _____.
    a. hunting and gathering bands
    b. horticultural tribes
    c. pastoral tribes
    d. a state type of political organization
    e. the household as the unit of production and consumption

15. A businessperson who wants to build a factory in the Middle East could benefit from the contributions of a cultural anthropologist. In which of the following ways would an anthropologist be likely to help?

    a. provide knowledge of the principles of market exchange

    b. introduce a new method of paying local workers

    c. tell the businessperson how to sit, dress, and talk when making the arrangements with local people

    d. screen workers who have diseases

    e. "introduce a new method of paying local workers", "tell the businessperson how to sit, dress, and talk when making the arrangements with local people"

16. An example of tribal leadership is the _____. Such men are leaders of a localized descent groups or of a territorial group.

    a. manager

    b. Big Man

    c. mayor

    d. shaman

    e. chairman

17. The group discussed in the article *Prestige Economics in Papua New Guinea*, was the _____.

    a. Kaluli

    b. Kapauku

    c. Enga

    d. Mekranoti

    e. Mende

18. Not only have anthropologists found niches for themselves in the world of business, but since 1972, the number of them going into business has grown _____.

    a. tenfold

    b. fivefold

    c. 50 percent

    d. anthropologists don't work in the business world

    e. 25 percent

19. One of the newest innovations in the market-research and design industry is _____.

    a. survey questionnaire

    b. telephone surveys

    c. ethnology

    d. ethnography

    e. case studies

20. In the original study "Prestige Economics in Papua New Guinea," it is stated that for Big Man feasts a surplus is created for the express purpose of gaining prestige through a display of wealth and generous giving of gifts-hence the term _____.

    a. surplus economy

    b. status economy

    c. festival economy

    d. prestige economy

    e. conspicuous consumption

21. One successful anthropologist working in corporate America doing international consulting for a large computer firm is _____.

    a. Vicki Cassman

    b. Jennifer Thompson

    c. Dureen Hughes

    d. Laura Nader

    e. Kathleen Gonzales

22. Not only have anthropologists found niches for themselves in the world of business, but since 1972, the number of them going into business has grown _____.

    a. twofold

    b. fourfold

    c. tenfold

    d. fivefold

    e. sevenfold

23. An anthropologist interested in the systems of production, exchange, and redistribution would be called a _____ anthropologist.

    a. political

    b. linguistic

    c. economic

    d. physical

    e. psychological

24. The sexual division of labor configuration that has been described as the flexible/integrated pattern is found among which of the following?

    a. Bakhtiari

    b. Ju/'hoansi

    c. Taiwanese

    d. Dahomeans

    e. Industrial countries

25. One example of specialization is afforded by the _____ people of Ethiopia's Danakil Depression. The men of this group are miners of salt.

    a. Nuer

    b. Azande

    c. Hadza

    d. Afar

    e. Ashanti

26. A societal obligation compelling a family to distribute goods so that no one accumulates more wealth than anyone else is referred to by anthropologists as a _____.

    a. flat tax

    b. commune

    c. capital gains tax

    d. poverty spreader

    e. leveling mechanism

27. In economic anthropology, a mode of exchange in which the value of the gift is not calculated, nor is the time of repayment specified is known as _____.

    a. charity

    b. generosity

    c. a handout

    d. generalized reciprocity

    e. Christmas

28. In political fund-raising in the United States large contributors expect that their "generosity" will buy influence with a candidate. What category of reciprocity would this fall under?

    a. derisive

    b. negative

    c. general

    d. balanced

    e. None of these

29. Not all trade is motivated by economic considerations. A classic case of this is _____.

    a. silent trade

    b. the swap meet

    c. the flea market

    d. the Kula ring

    e. the *cargo* system

30. Among the _____, both cacao beans and cotton cloaks served as money.
    a. Tiv
    b. Aztecs
    c. Enga
    d. Trobriand Islanders
    e. Inca

31. The Kula ring is a form of _____ that reinforces trade relations among a group of seafaring Melanesians inhabiting a ring of islands off the eastern coast of Papua New Guinea.
    a. negative reciprocity
    b. balanced reciprocity
    c. market exchange
    d. silent trade
    e. generalized reciprocity

32. _____ first described the Kula ring, he observed it during ethnographic research among the Trobriand Islanders between 1915-1918.
    a. Franz Boas
    b. Gordon Childe
    c. Bronislaw Malinowski
    d. Margaret Mead
    e. A.R. Radcliffe-Brown

33. Harvard-trained anthropologist _____ uses anthropological tools to research and analyze corporate "cultures" in order to help them solve problems and improve performance.
    a. Karen Stephenson
    b. Karen Harry
    c. Barbara Roth
    d. Jennifer Thompson
    e. Steve Barnett

True/False Practice Questions

1. According to Robert Lowie, patterns of reciprocity among the Crow did not involve women.
   True or False

2. In "silent trade," no words are spoken, but the participants must meet face to face to exchange goods.
   True or False

3. The Inca empire of Peru featured a highly efficient redistributive system.
   True or False

4. The economist responsible for the concept of "conspicuous consumption" was Thorsten Veblen.
   True or False

5. The Enga live in Indonesia.
   True or False

6. Jomo Kenyatta was an anthropologist who became "the father" of modern Kenya.
   True or False

7. The Big Man feasts exist merely as arenas for grandiose men to flaunt their ambition.
   True or False

8. Big Man feasts are like conspicuous consumption in Western societies; the emphasis is on the hoarding of goods which would make them unavailable to others.
   True or False

9. Anthropologists only work in exotic, faraway places like remote islands, deep forests, hostile deserts, or arctic wastelands.
   True or False

10. There is a potential job market for anthropologists in the market-research and design area.
    True or False

11. According to your textbook, most anthropologists who work at market-research and design companies are not really "doing ethnography."
    True or False

12. Doing research in corporate America is not so different from doing initial anthropological research in an unfamiliar culture.
    True or False

13. Trobriand Island men devote a great deal of time and energy to raise yams, not for themselves but to give to others.
    True or False

14. No specialization of labor craft exists in nonindustrial societies.
    True or False

15. Anthropologists have found no form of conspicuous consumption occurring in nonindustrial societies.
    True or False

16. In non-Western societies the market is an important focus of social as well as economic activity.
    True or False

17. In Africa, much of the farming is the job of women. Failure to accept this fact is responsible for the failure of many development schemes, since outside experts design projects that usually assume the men in society are the farmers.
    True or False

18. The Kula ring used to involve thousands of men but no longer functions today.
    True or False

19. Anthropological research methods work well when conducting cross-cultural research, but are worthless in studying the modern corporate way of life.
    True or False

20. Corporations headquartered in the so-called developed world are in business not only to make a profit, but to protect the weak, benefit the poor, support the sick, and save the environment.
    True or False

Practice Short Answer Questions

1. Describe and discuss the new form of market exchange that has developed in industrial and post-industrial societies.

2. What is meant by the term "savage capitalism?"

Practice Essays

1. Compare and contrast the different ideas about the nature and control of land that exist among food foragers, horticulturalists, pastoralists, intensive agriculturalists, and industrialists.

2. Compare and contrast the different ideas about tools and tool ownership in foraging, horticultural, and intensive agricultural societies.

3. Describe the ecological context of the "Big Man" system of the Enga.

4. Describe the prestige economies of the Enga. Explain their function and purpose.

5. Describe what an anthropologist can contribute to the world of business.

6. Compare and contrast a prestige economy with an economy based on conspicuous consumption.

7. Specify and elaborate on the three categories of distribution of material goods as classified by economist Karl Polanyi.

8. What is a "Big Man?" What role does he play in the prestige economies of Melanesia?

9. Because trade can be essential in the quest for survival and is often undertaken for the sake of luxury, people may go to grreat lengths to establish and maintain good trade relations. A classic example of this is the Kula ring. What is the Kula ring? Describe.

10. Discuss Karen Stephenson's work in corporate anthropology. How is her work different from the work of more traditional anthropologists?

11. Who was Jomo Kenyatta?

Solutions

Fill-in-the-Blank

1. production, exchange, redistribution

2. Ju /'hoansi

3. pastoralism, intensive agriculture

4. household

5. axe, digging stick, hoe

6. leveling mechanism

7. Karl Polyani

8. reciprocity, redistribution, exchange

9. redistribution

10. conspicuous consumption

11. clan

12. India

Multiple-Choice Practice Questions

1. B

2. E

3. B

4. C

5. B

6. A

7. B

8. C

9. C

10. C

11. D

12. D

13. B

14. D

15. E

16. B

17. C

18. B

19. D

20. D

21. C

22. D

23. C

24. B

25. D

26. E

27. D

28. D

29. D

30. B

31. B

32. C

33. A

True/False Practice Questions

1. F

2. F

3. T

4. T

5. F

6. T

7. F

8. F

9. F

10. T

11. T

12. T

13. T

14. F

15. F

16. T

17. T

18. F

19. F

20. F

Chapter 8

Sex and Marriage

Synopsis

Chapter 8 defines marriage as a system for regulating sexual access and explores the variations on the theme of marriage throughout the world. The interactions of marriage, social structure, and environment are considered.

What You Should Learn from This Chapter

I.   Understand what marriage is in nonethnocentric terms.

II.   Know the controls societies place on sexual relations and theories as to why these controls are necessary.

III. Understand the many forms of marriage and how they relate with other aspects of society:

    A.   monogamy

    B.   polygyny

    C.   polyandry

    D.   two forms of cousin marriage

IV.   Understand the role of consanguineal and affinal ties in society.

V.   Know the kinds of gift exchanges that often accompany marriage.

Key Terms and Names

affinal kin
bride price
bride service
Claude Levi-Strauss
conjugal bond
consanguineal kin
dowry
endogamy
exogamy
group marriage
incest taboo

levirate
marriage
matrilateral cross-cousin marriage
monogamy
nuclear family
patrilateral parallel-cousin marriage
polyandry
polygyny
serial monogamy
sororate

Exercise

1. Draw your family tree in the space below. Make it as extensive as you can without consulting any of your relatives. What accounts for the relatively truncated kindreds of most North Americans?

2. Briefly identify and locate the following cultures on the map.
A. Nayar
B. Nandi
C. Morocco
D. Tibet

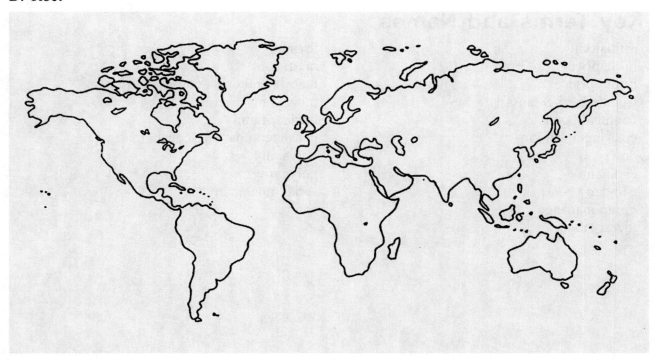

Exercise

Review Questions

1. Why are human females able to engage in sexual activity regardless of their ovulation cycles?

2. Why does sexual activity require social control?

3. Describe the sex life of the Trobrianders.

4. As discussed in your textbook, describe the traditional marriage system of the Nayar.

5. What is the incest taboo?

6. Why do people who live in close proximity to one another exhibit reduced sexual activity?

7. What are the Oedipus and Electra complexes?

8. How have geneticists attempted to explain the incest taboo?

9. Distinguish between endogamy and exogamy.

10. What were the initial reasons for exogamy, according to Tylor, Levi-Strauss, and Cohen?

11. Distinguish between marriage and mating.

12. To what extent can North American society be characterized as monogamous?

13. Provide a nonethnocentric definition of marriage.

14. Distinguish between consanguineal and conjugal families.

15. Distinguish between polygynous and polyandrous families.

16. What form of marriage does the majority of the world's societies exhibit?

17. Characterize the typical polygynous society.

18. What is the attitude of Kapauku women towards their husbands' other wives?

19. Describe the social and economic context of polyandry.

20. Discuss the contexts in which sororate, levirate, and serial monogamy are likely to occur.

21. What benefits do arranged marriages have?

22. Describe the marriage system of Sidi Embarek, Morocco.

23. Distinguish between patrilineal parallel-cousin and matrilineal cross-cousin marriage.

24. How is marriage exchange conducted among the Trobrianders?

25. Distinguish between bride price, dowry, and bride service.

26. What is the function of female-female marriage among the Nandi?

27. What role can anthropologists play in the study of AIDS?

Fill-in-the-Blank

1. Marriage is a cultural transaction that regulates men's and women's rights of _____ access to one another and defines the context in which women are eligible to bear children.

2. The female ability to engage is sexual relations at any time is related to the development of _____ locomotion among the hominines.

3. Only about _____ percent of the world's societies prohibit all sexual involvement outside of marriage.

4. The bond between two individuals joined by marriage is called a(n) _____ bond.

5. Households composed only of "blood" relatives are said to contain _____ kin.

6. The _____ taboo prohibits sexual relations between specified individuals.

7. _____ is a rule mandating the one marry outside of a particular group, while _____ mandates marriage within the group.

8. In the United States, _____ is the only legally recognized form of marriage, but some Americans do engage in other forms.

9. A _____ family contains a husband and his multiple wives, while a _____ family contains a wife and her multiple husbands.

10. Among the Turkana of northern Kenya, _____ is the preferred form of marriage.

11. When the wives in a polygynous marriage are sisters, this is called _____ polygyny.

12. _____ marriage refers to a marriage in which several men and women have sexual access to one another.

13. In a _____ , a widow marries the brother of her deceased husband; in a _____ , a widower marries the sister of his deceased wife.

14. Marrying a sequence of partners throughout one's life is called _____ .

15. In a patrilateral parallel-cousin marriage, a boy marries his father's _____ daughter.

16. _____ is a gift exchange occurring at marriage in which money or goods are transferred from the groom's side to the bride's.

17. In a _____ system, the bride's family provides money or goods at the time of marriage.

18. The Nandi of western Kenya practice a form of marriage in which a woman marries _____ .

19. Divorce rates in Western society are considered high by many people but are low compared to divorce rates among _____ societies.

20. _____ is a French anthropologist who launched a school of thought called structuralism.

21. Medical anthropologists can contribute significantly to the study of _____ and _____ through investigating the social and sexual contexts of disease transmission in various societies.

Multiple-Choice Practice Questions

1. _____ is a transaction in which a woman and man establish a continuing claim to the right of sexual access to one another, and in which the woman involved becomes eligible to bear children.

   a. Family

   b. Marriage

   c. Incest

   d. Affinity

   e. Sex

2. One explanation for the tendency of human females to be sexually receptive on a continuing basis is that _____.

   a. it is an accidental byproduct of the high hormone requirements for persistent bipedal locomotion.

   b. it increases competitiveness among the males of a group.

   c. it encourages endogamy

   d. it discourages incest

   e. it leads to greater competitiveness among women

3. Marriage resolves the problem of how to bring sexual activity under _____ control.

   a. biological

   b. male

   c. cultural

   d. female

   e. mother-in-law

4. A household composed of married people contains _____ kin.

   a. affinal

   b. consanguineal

   c. endogamous

   d. nuclear

   e. instinctive

5. According to the _____ theory of incest taboo, children feel so guilty about their sexual feelings for a parent that they repress them, and this is expressed culturally in the incest taboo.

   a. genetic

   b. instinctive

   c. psychological

   d. anthropological

   e. sociological

6. Although all societies have some kind of incest taboo, the relationship that is considered incestuous may vary. Concepts of incest seem to be related to a group's definitions of endogamy and exogamy, thus suggesting that incest taboos may help to promote _____.

   a. alliances between groups

   b. inbreeding

   c. brother-sister marriages

   d. parallel-cousin marriages

   e. cross-cousin marriages

7. Marriage within a particular group of individuals is called _____.

   a. incest

   b. exogamy

   c. monogamy

   d. endogamy

   e. polygamy

8. The French anthropologist Claude Levi-Strauss says that the incest taboo is universal because humans _____.

   a. are instinctively opposed to inbreeding

   b. repress their sexual desire for the parent of the opposite sex

   c. have learned to establish alliances with strangers and thereby share and develop culture

   d. prefer to marry their brothers and sisters

   e. don't like sex

9. A residential kin group composed of a woman, her dependent children, and at least one adult male joined through marriage or blood relationship is a/an _____.

   a. family

   b. conjugal bond

   c. endogamous

   d. nuclear family

   e. serial marriage

10. Families can be consanguineal or conjugal. The conjugal family has many forms. One type of conjugal family is the _____, consisting of the husband, wife, and dependent children.

    a. polygynous family

    b. polygamous family

    c. polyandrous family

    d. nuclear family

    e. extended family

11. Although _____ may statistically be the most common form of marriage around the world, it is not the most preferred.

    a. polygyny

    b. monogamy

    c. polyandry

    d. polygamy

    e. the levirate

12. Polygyny _____.
    a. means marriage to more than one man
    b. is the most common form of marriage
    c. is usually possible only when a man is fairly wealthy
    d. is less common than polyandry
    e. is an example of group marriage

13. An example of group marriage would be _____.
    a. a pastoral nomad's wife among the Turkana who actively searches for another woman to share her husband and her work with the livestock.
    b. the Moonies having a large wedding ceremony at which five hundred couples, each one assigned to another, are married at the same time.
    c. a prosperous member of the Kapauku in western New Guinea who is able to afford a bride price for four wives.
    d. a hippy commune in the Haight-Ashbury district in which it is accepted that all adult members of the commune have sexual access to each other.
    e. a Nayar household in which a woman takes several lovers.

14. The levirate and the sororate _____.
    a. are secret societies, like sororities and fraternities.
    b. function to maintain the relationship between the family of the bride and the family of the groom.
    c. are *usually* possible only when the man is fairly wealthy
    d. are types of cattle in pastoralist societies
    e. exist only in advanced industrial societies

15. Serial monogamy tends to occur in societies where _____.
    a. a woman with children receives a great deal of help from her mother and brothers
    b. women do not have many children
    c. a woman with dependent children, isolated from her parents, marries a series of partners to get the assistance of another adult
    d. women are very wealthy
    e. divorce is forbidden

16. The main function of a bride price is _____.
    a. for a man to show off to his wife how rich he is
    b. for a man to buy a slave
    c. for the wife's people to gain prestige in the village
    d. to compensate the wife's family for her labor
    e. for the wife's people to buy a husband for their daughter

17. When a man marries his father's brother's daughter in ancient Greece or traditional China, _____

    a. he is committing incest
    b. he is practicing matrilineal cross-cousin marriage
    c. he is practicing patrilateral parallel-cousin marriage
    d. he is keeping property within the single male line of descent
    e. "he is practicing patrilateral parallel-cousin marriage", "he is keeping property within the single male line of descent"

18. In which of the following situations would you expect to find the custom of bride price?

    a. A bride and groom leave the community after marriage and set up their own household in a distant city
    b. A bride and groom go to live with the bride's people
    c. A bride and groom go to live with the groom's people
    d. A bride and groom go to live with the bride's mother's brother
    e. none of these

19. When the economy is based on _____ and where the man does most of the productive work, the bride's people may give a dowry that protects the woman against desertion and is a statement of her economic status.

    a. food foraging
    b. pastoralism
    c. intensive agriculture
    d. horticulture
    e. industrialism

20. The woman/woman marriage custom found in sub-Saharan Africa _____.

    a. enables a woman without sons to inherit a share of her husband's property
    b. confers legitimacy on the children of a woman who had been unable to find a husband
    c. enables the woman who adopts a male identity to raise her status
    d. enables the woman who is the wife of the female husband to raise her status and live a more secure life
    e. "enables a woman without sons to inherit a share of her husband's property", "confers legitimacy on the children of a woman who had been unable to find a husband.", "enables the woman who adopts a male identity to raise her status" and "enables the woman who is the wife of the female husband to raise her status and live a more secure life"

21. Which of the following constitutes a culturally valid reason for divorce among different groups?

    a. sterility or impotence
    b. cruelty
    c. being a poor provider
    d. being a lazy housekeeper
    e. "sterility or impotence", "cruelty", "being a poor provider" and "being a lazy housekeeper"

22. In an arranged marriage in India, the newly married couple will go to live in a _____ family.

    a. nuclear

    b. combined

    c. mixed

    d. joint

    e. consanguine

23. According to the article in your textbook "Arranging Marriage in India," among urban Indians an important source of contacts in trying to arrange a marriage is/are the _____.

    a. social club.

    b. newspaper personals

    c. internet chat rooms

    d. match making businesses

    e. temple

24. Which of the following characteristics would be most important in an Indian family's selection of a bride for their son?

    a. good looks

    b. well-educated

    c. independent

    d. have higher social status

    e. good character

25. _____ is the leading exponent of French structuralism.

    a. Bronislaw Malinowski

    b. Franz Boas

    c. Claude Levi-Strauss

    d. Phillipe Cousteau

    e. Emile Durkiem

26. What sets _____ apart is that sex may occur even when the female is not swollen.

    a. chimpanzees

    b. bonobos

    c. macaques

    d. orangutangs

    e. gorillas

27. According to Haviland, in the United States there are somewhere between 20,000 and
    _____ people in the Rocky Mountain states that live in households made up of a man
    with two or more wives.

    a. 100,000

    b. 75,000

    c. 15,000

    d. 1 million

    e. 60,000

28. In _____, the state legislature recently passed, and the governor signed, a bill that permits
    same-sex partners to enjoy all the benefits of marriage.

    a. California

    b. Delaware

    c. New Hampshire

    d. Massachusetts

    e. Vermont

29. No societies have achieved greater separation between the sexual and reproductive attributes of
    women than the _____.

    a. Nandi

    b. Nayar

    c. Azande

    d. Mundugamor

    e. the United States and other Western countries

30. _____ saw exogamy as the basis of a distinction between early hominine life isolated
    endogamous groups and of the *Homo sapiens* in a supportive society with an accumulating
    culture.

    a. R.M. Keesing

    b. Claude Levi-Strauss

    c. Yehudi Cohen

    d. Edward Sapir

    e. Clyde Kluckhohn

31. In the United States, as in most Western countries, _____ is the only legally recognized
    form of marriage.

    a. polygamy

    b. polygyny

    c. monogamy

    d. polyandry

    e. serial

32. Most divorced people in the United States remarry at least once. Thus, _____ is not uncommon.

    a. polygamy

    b. serial monogamy

    c. sororate marriage

    d. levirate marriage

    e. polyandry

33. Conjugal families are formed on the basis of marital ties between husband and wife. Which of the following are forms of conjugal families?

    a. polyandrous families

    b. consanguine families

    c. polygynous families

    d. nuclear families

    e. polyandrous families, polygynous families and nuclear families

34. In some societies when a woman marries she receives her share of the family inheritance, or her _____.

    a. bride price

    b. bride service

    c. dowry

    d. bride commission

    e. birthright

35. Among the _____ of Kenya, sterility or impotence were grounds for divorce.

    a. Eritreans

    b. Gusii

    c. Nandi

    d. Hutu

    e. Chenchu

36. In some societies, preferred marriages are a man marrying his father's brother's daughter. This is known as patrilateral parallel-cousin marriage. Although not obligatory, such marriages have been favored historically among which of the following cultures?

    a. traditional Chinese

    b. Arabs

    c. ancient Greece

    d. ancient Israelites

    e. traditional Chinese, Arabs, ancient Greece and ancient Israelites

37. Only a minority of known societies, about _____ percent, have rules requiring that sexual involvement take place only within marriage.
    a. 25
    b. 15
    c. 10
    d. 5
    e. 30

38. In which of the following countries is same-sex marriages considered socially acceptable and allowed by law?
    a. Mexico
    b. Canada
    c. Italy
    d. the Netherlands
    e. B and D

39. A culturally sanctioned union between two or more persons that established certain rights and obligations between the persons, between them and their children, and between them and their in-laws.
    a. monogamy
    b. conjugal bond
    c. endogamy
    d. exogamy
    e. marriage

True/False Practice Questions

1. Trobriand children begin sexual experimentation at a young age.
    True or False

2. About half of the world's societies prohibit sexual involvement outside of marriage.
    True or False

3. Haviland believes that evidence on intrafamily homicides support Freud's theories of the Oedipus and Electra complex.
    True or False

4. Brother-sister marriages were common among farmers in Roman Egypt.
    True or False

5. Primate evidence shows that it is likely that humans started out as a monogamous species.
    True or False

6. People want pretty much the same things in marriage whether it is in India or America.
    True or False

7. Today, a dowry is expected by law in India.
    True or False

8. In India it is understood that matches (marriages) would be arranged only within the same caste and general social class.
   True or False

9. In India no crossing of subcastes is permissible even if the class positions of the bride's and groom's families are similar.
   True or False

10. As far as arranging a marriage is concerned, in India the basic rule seems to be that a family's reputation is most important.
    True or False

11. Although it is common for the newly married Indian couple to go live with the groom's joint family in the rural area, it is not common among the urban, upper-middle class in India.
    True or False

12. In India divorce is still a scandal and thus the divorce rate is exceedingly low.
    True or False

13. When arranging an Indian marriage consideration of a girl's looks are more important than her character.
    True or False

14. In an arranged marriage in India a woman is being judged as a prospective daughter- in-law as much as a prospective bride.
    True or False

15. In an arranged Indian marriage, offering the proper gifts is often an important factor in influencing the relationship between the bride's and groom's families, and the treatment of the bride in her new home.
    True or False

16. In India a military career with its economic security has great prestige and is considered a benefit in finding a suitable bride.
    True or False

17. While a boy's skin color is a less important consideration than a girl's, it is still a factor when arranging a marriage in India.
    True or False

18. Bonobos will not engage in sex when a female is pregnant.
    True or False

19. Both cross-cultural studies, and those of other animals, suggest that homosexual behavior is unnatural.
    True or False

20. In a number of societies researchers have discovered that same-sex marriages are regarded as perfectly appropriate.
    True or False

21. Among primates, in general, monogamous mating patterns are not common.
    True or False

22. In the United States today, single-parent households outnumber nuclear family households.
    True or False

23. The obsession with a particular idea of feminine beauty in the United States is reflected in the beauty pageants organized for very young girls.
    True or False

24. Divorce is possible in all societies, though reasons for divorce as well as its frequency vary widely from one society to another.
    True or False

25. There are no cultures that prescribe male-to-male sexual acts, for any reason.
    True or False

26. The social rules and cultural meanings of all sexual behavior are subject to great variability from one society to another.
    True or False

27. Marriage, as pointed out in your textbook, always involves the establishment of a new family.
    True or False

Practice Matching

Match the culture with its characteristic.

1. _____ Nandi
2. _____ Moroccans
3. _____ Nayar
4. _____ Tibetans
5. _____ North Americans

a. A culture emphasizing love and choice as a basis for marriage.
b. South Indian people who give the mother's brothers key responsibility in child rearing.
c. Patrilineal North African people who practice arranged marriage.
d. East African pastoralists who practice woman/woman marriage.
e. Polyandrous society of central Asia.

Short Answer Practice Questions

1. What is the positive outcome of having strict religious rules that regulate sexual relations?

2. Explain why your textbook's definition of marriage refers to "persons" rather than "a man and a woman."

Practice Essays

1. Discuss how various societies have sought to regulate sexual relations.

2. Explain the universality of the incest taboo and describe its cross-cultural variation.

3. Describe how the "romantic love" complex impacts North American marriage patterns. Is romantic love involved in marriage in India? Discuss why or why not?

4. What factors affect the stability of marriages and the choice of mates?

5. What factors must be taken into consideration when arranging a marriage in India? Describe.

6. Describe the contributions of anthropologists to our understanding and control of AIDS.

7. Describe the Nayar and their rules of sexual access.

8. Anthropologists have found that universally societies have cultural rules that act to control sexual relations. What are the rules of sexual access from one culture to another?

9. What is the "incest taboo?" Explain why is it such a challenge for anthropologists to explain in terms of its universality and why incest commonly should be regarded as such loathsome behavior?

10. Explain the distinction between marriage and mating.

11. Discuss the arrangement of marriage in India.

12. Expound on the reasons and frequency of divorce from society to society.

Solutions

Fill-in-the-Blank

1. sexual
2. bipedal
3. five
4. conjugal
5. consanguineal
6. incest
7. Exogamy, endogamy
8. monogamy
9. polygynous, polyandrous
10. polygamy
11. sororal
12. Group
13. levirate, sororate
14. serial marriage
15. brother's
16. Bride price
17. dowery
18. woman
19. matrilineal
20. Claude Levi-Strauss
21. HIV, AIDs

Multiple-Choice Practice Questions

1. B
2. A
3. C
4. A
5. C
6. A
7. D
8. C
9. A
10. D
11. B
12. C
13. D
14. B
15. C
16. D
17. E
18. C
19. C
20. E
21. E
22. D
23. A
24. E
25. C
26. B
27. E
28. E
29. E
30. B
31. C
32. B
33. E
34. C
35. B
36. E
37. B
38. E
39. E

True/False Practice Questions

1. T
2. F
3. F
4. T
5. F
6. F
7. F
8. T
9. F
10. T
11. F
12. T
13. F
14. T
15. T
16. F
17. T
18. F
19. F
20. T
21. T
22. T
23. T
24. T
25. F
26. T
27. F

Practice Matching

1. D
2. C

3. B

4. E

5. A

Chapter 9

Family and Household

Synopsis

Chapter 9 focuses on the differences between families and households, noting that the Western assumption that all households are built around conjugal relationships is ethnocentric. The major residence patterns are defined, and the various problems created by different kinds of living arrangements are explored.

What You Should Learn from This Chapter

I. Understand the functions of the family in human society and the difference between family and household.

II. Know the various forms of family organization and the difficulties associated with each:

    A.   polygynous

    B.   extended

    C.   nuclear

    D.   female-headed

III. Know the basic kinds of residence rules that are found in diverse societies:

    A.   patrilocal

    B.   matrilocal

    C.   neolocal

Key Terms

conjugal family
consanguine family
extended family
family
family of orientation
family of procreation

household
matrilocal residence
neolocal residence
nuclear family
patrilocal residence

Exercises

1. Anthropologists have developed a method of expressing kin relationships symbolically. In this form of notation, males are represented by triangles and females by circles. A bond of marriage is represented by an equal sign (two parallel lines) while a consanguineal bond is represented by a single line. For example, the following diagram shows a conventional nuclear family of a husband, wife, and two children:

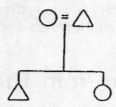

There are further specifications possible in the standard genealogical notation. If an individual is deceased, he or she is represented by a diagonal line drawn through the triangle or circle. Here is a diagram of a widow with her three sons and one daughter. In the society in which this hypothetical family lives, goods are inherited through the female line, from mother to daughter. This is indicated on the diagram by coloring in the triangles and circles in the line of inheritance (the lineage).

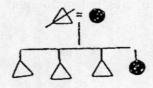

Sometimes other kinds of modifications can be added to a genealogical chart as well. For example, a residence group might be indicated by drawing a line around the individuals included in the household. The following shows an extended family household based on ties between brothers.

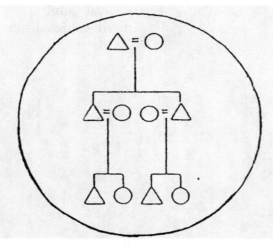

Now redraw your family tree from Chapter 8 using standard genealogical notation. (Don't worry about inheritance or residence here; just diagram the basic affinal and consanguineal ties).

2. On the three charts below, illustrate a ***patrilocal*** residence group, a ***matrilocal*** residence group, and an ***avunculocal*** residence group by drawing a line around the included individuals.

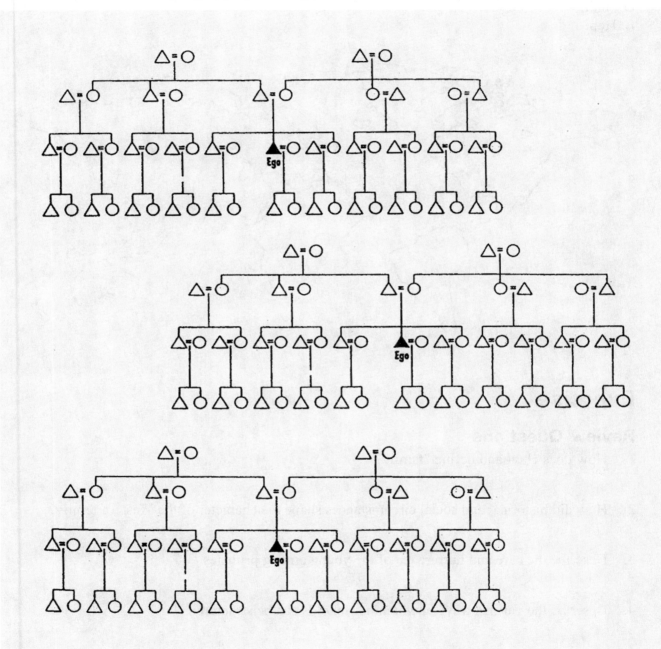

3. Briefly identify and locate the following cultures:
A. Mundurucu
B. Tory Islanders
C. Coastal Mainers
D. Inuit
E. Hopi

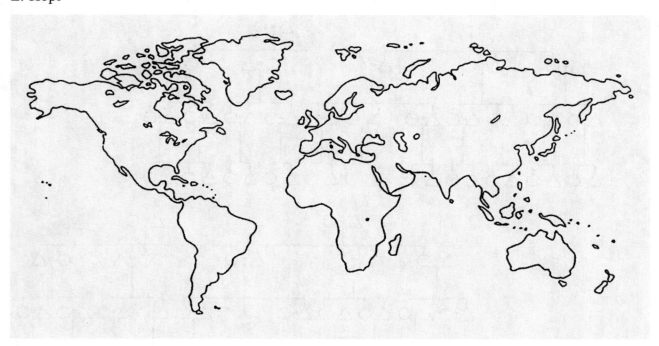

Exercise

Review Questions

1. How does Haviland define "family?"

2. How did historical and social circumstances shape the character of the Western family?

3. Describe the care and nurturance of the young among primates.

4. Describe the various ways in which households can be structured.

5. How is the modern American family related to the rise of industrial capitalism?

6. Describe the nuclear family.

7. What relations might be a part of the extended family?

8. What societal factors might contribute to the existence of extended families?

9. Distinguish the five common patterns of residence.

10. How does ecology impact residence pattern?

11. What residence pattern was traditionally followed by people along the Maine coast and why?

12. What residence pattern was traditionally followed by the Hopi and how did it influence family life?

13. What problems may accompany polygynous families and how are they handled?

14. What problems may accompany extended families and how are they resolved?

15. What problems may accompany nuclear families and how are they worked out?

16. What problems may accompany female-headed families and how are they dealt with?

17. Why did the patriarchal colonial family fade away over time?

18. How does the status of women relate to various kinds of family and residence patterns?

Fill-in-the-Blank
1. The independent nuclear family emerged in Europe in the fourth century A.D. in response to regulations put forward by _____ .
2. The "ever-changing family in North America" was studied by _____ .
3. A family based on a marital tie is called a _____ family, while a family based on blood ties is called a _____ family.

4. A _____ is a residential group composed of a woman, her dependent children, and at least one male joined through marriage or a blood relationship.

5. Among the Mundurucu, after age thirteen boys go to live in _____ .

6. Two examples of the rare consanguineal family are the _____ and the _____ .

7. Two examples of societies based on independent nuclear families are the _____ and the _____ .

8. In a _____ form of residence, husbands go to live with their wife's parents after marriage.

9. In a _____ form of residence, wives go to live with their husband's parents after marriage.

10. The Hopi practice _____ residence while the Chinese practice _____ residence.

11. Among the Trobrianders, a newly married couple goes to live with the groom's mother's brother. This is called _____ residence.

12. The Mbuti practice _____ residence.

13. During colonial times _____ children were treated much like servants, especially if they were of the same or similar age.

Multiple-Choice Practice Questions

1. The independent nuclear family in Europe _____.
   a. emerged recently as the result of regulations passed by the Roman Catholic Church in the fourth century A.D.
   b. is a universal family form that is natural to primates
   c. is found only in Europe and places to which Europeans have emigrated
   d. is found only in non-Western societies
   e. was the only form of family considered legitimate in the Old Testament of the Bible

2. The effect of industrialization on nuclear families was _____.
   a. an increased dependence on extended kin, who could provide aid during difficult times
   b. greater isolation because of the mobility required of an industrial labor force
   c. greater conflict among members of the nuclear family over scarce jobs
   d. the tendency to develop polygyny
   e. the tendency to develop the levirate

3. Which of the following statements is **correct**?
   a. The period of infant dependency in humans is the same as that in other primates
   b. The family is the only unit in which children can be reared in a nurturant manner
   c. Only among humans are males larger and stronger than females
   d. Human infants can survive only with the care provided by the biological mother
   e. none of these

4. A household is _____.
    a. a residential group composed of a woman, her dependent children, and at least one male
    b. joined through marriage or consanguineal relationship
    c. a nonresidential group composed of people who share common interests
    d. a residential unit within which economic production, consumption, inheritance, child rearing and shelter are organized and carried out
    e. a temporary association of strangers
    f. a research center

5. A residential kin group composed of related women, their brothers, and the women's offspring is _____.
    a. a conjugal family
    b. an extended family
    c. a consanguineal family
    d. a nuclear family
    e. a patrilocal family

6. What do traditional Inuit society and contemporary North American society have in common that explains the similarity in their family structure?
    a. Both developed in arctic environments
    b. Both rely on the technology of hunting
    c. In both, people have very few possessions so there is little jealousy
    d. Both care for their elderly
    e. Both are highly mobile

7. The _____ is composed of people related to each other by ties of blood who bring their spouses to live in the family.
    a. extended family
    b. polygamous family
    c. consanguine family
    d. nuclear family
    e. communal family

8. Residence patterns refer to _____.
    a. how a group makes it's living in a particular environment
    b. the structure of a family under certain ecological conditions
    c. where a couple chooses to live after they are married
    d. the problems that different families have
    e. whether the husband and wife sleep in the same room or in different rooms after they are married

9. Societies that rely on animal husbandry or intensive agriculture, in which polygyny is customary and where warfare is prominent enough to make male cooperation important, are most likely to practice _____ residence.

    a. matrilocal

    b. avunculocal

    c. ambilocal

    d. patrilocal

    e. neolocal

10. Ambilocal residence is found in societies _____.

    a. that stress the cooperation of women

    b. where warfare is common and men wield authority

    c. where economic activity occurs outside the family, and families have to move frequently in search of jobs

    d. where males control property but descent and inheritance are reckoned through women

    e. where the nuclear family is not sufficient to handle the economic activities required for the family's survival, but resources are limited

11. Neolocal residence is common in industrial societies like our own because _____.

    a. newlyweds do not usually get along with their in-laws

    b. industries require workers to be able to move to wherever there are jobs

    c. most families set up their own businesses, and they do not require the labor of other family members outside the nuclear family

    d. brothers need to stay together for purposes of conducting warfare

    e. women continue to live with their brothers after marriage

12. Which of the following statements about residence patterns in the Trobriand Islands is **incorrect**?

    a. All couples live with the husband's mother's brother

    b. Men who are in line to take over control of their descent group's assets will take their wives to live with their mother's brother

    c. Most couples live patrilocally

    d. Men who live with their fathers gain access to land controlled by their fathers' descent groups

    e. Men who live with their fathers also have access to land controlled through female descent

13. A man who marries several sisters is practicing _____.

    a. avunculocal residence

    b. sororal polygyny

    c. fraternal polyandry

    d. infidelity.

    e. matrilocal residence

14. Extended families usually work more effectively if authority is in the hands of one person, such as the eldest son. Which of the following methods of reducing conflict between this eldest son and his younger brothers are likely to be found in extended families?

    a. moving out of the household

    b. dependence training

    c. independence training

    d. increasing the number of wives for the younger sons

    e. murder of the eldest son

15. Extended families have which of the following problems?

    a. loneliness caused by isolation from kin

    b. Children are raised to be independent, which competes with group harmony

    c. The eldest son is in competition with his younger brothers for the position of authority in the household

    d. mothers-in-law are powerless

    e. mother's brother is the authority figure

16. What are some of the problems associated with the nuclear family?

    a. Husbands and wives tend to be isolated from their kin

    b. There are no clear-cut lines of authority and rules for making decisions

    c. The elderly cannot depend on their children for aid when they are too old to take care of themselves

    d. There is very little privacy

    e. "Husbands and wives tend to be isolated from their kin". "There are no clear-cut lines of authority and rules for making decisions" and "The elderly cannot depend on their children for aid when they are too old to take care of themselves"

17. The increase in number of single-parent households headed by women is likely to be associated with _____.

    a. increased child support being paid by fathers

    b. increased participation of extended kin in caring for the children

    c. increased number of women below the poverty line

    d. decreased number of welfare programs

    e. decreased number of women below the poverty line in third-world countries

18. In the original 13 colonies people lived in households, each typically consisting of _____.

    a. an extended family

    b. a nuclear family

    c. the mother's brother's family

    d. the father's sister's family

    e. a clan

19. In her book on the history of American families, _____ wrote that "The central room or hall was where work, meals, play, religious instruction, and often sleep took place......."

    a. Coontz

    b. Galloway

    c. Cott

    d. Mead

    e. Benedict

20. Single parent households headed by women have been known and studied for a long time in the _____.

    a. countries of southern Europe

    b. country of India

    c. countries of Central America

    d. countries of the Caribbean basin

    e. countries of sub-Saharan Africa

21. In colonial North America people freely intruded into one another's households, and the affairs of all were carefully monitored and regulated by which of the following?

    a. village officials

    b. family members

    c. friends of the family

    d. church officials

    e. village officials and church officials

22. Colonial women were clearly subordinate, but a colonial woman's subordination was seen as a social necessity, **not** as a unique female condition caused by her _____.

    a. enculturation

    b. assimilation

    c. biology

    d. culture

    e. natural passivity

23. In some areas of colonial North America, such as the South (U.S.) and New France (Quebec), _____ marriage was practiced in order to consolidate land and transmit wealth in family lines.

    a. cousin

    b. sibling

    c. common-law

    d. same-sex

    e. arranged

24. As the patriarchal colonial family faded away, there was a general trend toward increasing
    _____.

    a. wealth

    b. privacy

    c. openness

    d. equality

    e. immorality

25. During the late 18th and early 19th centuries, a middle-class woman went to work outside the home for which of the following reasons?

    a. widowhood

    b. unemployment of the husband

    c. to purchase desired items

    d. to help with family expenses

    e. widowhood and unemployment of the husband

26. Which of the following did **not** occur to the population of the United States after the end of World War II?

    a. the age of marriage dropped

    b. fertility rose

    c. divorce declined

    d. the middle class moved to the suburbs

    e. women's participation in the work force decreased

27. From the early 1970s to the late 1990s, the percentage of children living with single parents rose from 4.7 percent to _____ percent.

    a. 18.2

    b. 25

    c. 50

    d. 10.4

    e. 15.5

28. The nuclear family, consisting of a married family and dependent children, is held up as the ideal in the United States. However, only _____ percent of U.S. households now conform to the independent nuclear family ideal.

    a. 50

    b. 26

    c. 11

    d. 5

    e. 15

29. The form of conjugal family most familiar to most North Americans is the independent nuclear family. This type of family is also apt to be prominent in societies such as the _____ that live in harsh environments.

    a. Bakhtiari

    b. Bantu

    c. Inuit

    d. Mekranoti Kayapo

    e. Gururumba

30. In the United States the extended family still exists in some places like along the _____.

    a. the Pacific Northwest coast

    b. the southern California coast

    c. the Mississippi River

    d. the Maine coast

    e. the shores of Lake Michigan

31. _____ residence is particularly well suited to situations where economic cooperation of more people than available in the nuclear family is needed, but where resources are limited in some way.

    a. Patrilocal

    b. Matrilocal

    c. Neolocal

    d. Ambilocal

    e. Avunculocal

32. Which of the following is **not a** circumstance related to the specific form a family takes?

    a. social

    b. historical

    c. biological

    d. ecological

    e. none of these

33. The nuclear family, consisting of a married family and dependent offspring, is held up as the ideal in which of the following societies?

    a. Tory Islanders

    b. Nayar

    c. Inuit

    d. United States

    e. Inuit and United States

34. The problems that arise in neolocal families are especially difficult in North American society because of which of the following?

    a. inequality that still persists between men and women

    b. the great emphasis placed on individualism and competition

    c. the absence of clearly understood patterns of responsibility between husbands and wives

    d. a clear model for child rearing

    e. "inequality that still persists between men and women", "the great emphasis placed on individualism and competition", "the absence of clearly understood patterns of responsibility between husbands and wives" and "a clear model for child rearing"

35. According to a cross-cultural survey of family types in 193 cultures around the world, the _____family is the most common.

    a. nuclear

    b. blended

    c. polygamous

    d. extended

    e. matrilocal

36. The family into which someone is born or adopted and raised anthropologists call the _____.

    a. extended family.

    b. blended family.

    c. family of procreation.

    d. family of orientation.

    e. conjugal family.

37. In _____villages, the men all live together in one house with all boys over the age of 13.

    a. Mundurucu

    b. Yanomami

    c. Inuit

    d. Nayar

    e. Watusi

38. Among the _____, married men and women are members of separate households, meeting periodically for sexual activity.

    a. Yoruba

    b. Musuo

    c. Lakota

    d. Bantu

    e. Nayar

39. In North America and parts of Europe, increasing numbers of people live in non-family households, either alone or with non-relatives. In fact, some _____% of households in the United States fall into this category.

    a. 50

    b. 22

    c. 14

    d. 32

    e. 75

True/False Practice Questions

1. A woman who marries several brothers is practicing sororal polygyny.
    True or False

2. Neolocal residence is common when the nuclear family must be able to move independently.
    True or False

3. Among the Mundurucu, the men's houses and the women's houses constitute separate families.
    True or False

4. Among the Hopi, daughters brought their husbands to live near their mother's house.
    True or False

5. In an avunculocal residence pattern, the newly married couple goes to live with the bride's father's sister.
    True or False

6. During colonial times few households contained people who were not kin to one another.
    True or False

7. Households in colonial America, much like today in some parts of the United States, privacy was of paramount importance.
    True or False

8. Unlike the way "the home" was seen in colonial North America, today in most households, "the home" is seen as a retreat from the stress and strain of the outside world.
    True or False

9. The colonial household was a center of economic production with no clear division between the public and the private.
    True or False

10. Colonial women constantly argued for equal status with colonial men.
    True or False

11. Female headed households are in fact a pathological response to economic restraints in U.S. society.
    True or False

12. Single parent households headed by women are relatively rare and are restricted to industrialized societies like the United States.
    True or False

13. Women constitute the majority of the poor, the underprivileged and the economically and socially disadvantaged in most of the world's societies, just as is becoming the case in the U.S.
    True or False

14. Colonial women did not need to grapple with reasons for their lack of equal status, since equal status was not even a social value for men.
    True or False

15. The concept of "face" may constitute a particularly potent check on children of extended families.
    True or False

16. More women than ever in the United States and abroad find themselves much better off than they were a decade ago.
    True or False

17. In the United States and Canada it is not considered desirable for young people to live with their parents beyond a certain age.
    True or False

18. The form of the family is basically the same from culture to culture.
    True or False

19. How men and women in other societies live together must be studied as logical outcomes of people's experience living in particular times, places, and social situations.
    True or False

20. Going it alone, single mothers are far more likely to face poverty than single fathers.
    True or False

Practice Matching

Match the culture with its characteristic.

1. _____ Inuit
2. _____ Coastal Mainers
3. _____ Mundurucu
4. _____ Tory Islanders
5. _____ Hopi

a. Irish society centered on consanguineal families.
b. Amazon people with "men's houses."
c. Americans maintaining an extended family tradition.
d. Southwestern Native Americans with families headed by women.
e. Arctic people who live in nuclear families.

Practice Short Answer Questions

1. Since 1950 the number of households headed by divorced, separated, and never-married individuals has grown significantly. What factors are responsible for this situation? Explain.

2. How do anthropologists define the household?

3. Describe the forms a family may take in today's world.

Practice Essays

1. Senator Daniel Patrick Moynihan was the author of a classic study on the problems of urban black people in the United States. Known as "the Moynihan Report," this document blamed irresponsible males and the resultant female-headed families for many of the ills that plague the African-American community. How might an anthropologist respond to this claim? (In fact, an anthropologist did respond to it. Her name is Carol Stack and her book *All Our Kin* was a significant landmark in our understanding of African-American culture. You might like to have a look at both the Moynihan Report and *All Our Kin* to see how anthropological insights can contribute to more appropriate government policies.)

2. Coontz suggests that the ideal American family as portrayed in the television series "Leave it to Beaver" is largely a myth. Explain why she has arrived at that conclusion.

3. Identify and discuss the problems inherent in the "traditional" nuclear family.

4. Discuss why the family today in the United States has become a matter of controversy and concern.

5. Where some form of conjugal or extended family is the norm, family exogamy requires that either the husband or wife, if not both, must move to a new household upon marriage. Describe the five most common patterns of residence open to newlyweds in extended families.

6. Explain how the family, as it has emerged in all corners of the world, is the product of particular historical and social circumstances.

7. Describe the parallels that exist between the nuclear family in industrial societies and families living under especially harsh environmental conditions.

Solutions

Fill-in-the-Blank

1. the Catholic Church
2. Coontz
3. conjugal, consanguineal
4. household
5. one house
6. Nayar, Tory Islanders
7. United States, Inuit
8. matrilocal
9. patrilocal
10. matrilocal, patrilocal
11. avunculocal
12. neolocal
13. biological

Multiple-Choice Practice Questions

1. A
2. B
3. E
4. C
5. C
6. E
7. A
8. C
9. D
10. E
11. B
12. A
13. B
14. B
15. C
16. E
17. C
18. B
19. A
20. D
21. E
22. C
23. A
24. B
25. E
26. E
27. A
28. B
29. C
30. D
31. D
32. C
33. E
34. E
35. D
36. D
37. A
38. E
39. D

True/False Practice Questions

1. F
2. T
3. F
4. T
5. F
6. F
7. F
8. T
9. T
10. F
11. F
12. F
13. T
14. T
15. F
16. F
17. T
18. F
19. T
20. T

Practice Matching

1. E
2. C
3. B
4. A
5. D

Chapter 10

Kinship and Descent

Synopsis

Chapter 10 presents some key concepts relating to the anthropological study of kinship and descent. The relationship of kinship patterns to other elements of social organization is explored.

What You Should Learn from This Chapter

I.   Know the difference between kindreds and lineal descent groups.

II.   Understand the various types of descent systems:

    A.   patrilineal

    B.   matrilineal

    C.   double descent

    D.   ambilineal

III.   Understand the organization and function of descent groups:

    A.   lineage

    B.   clan

    C.   phratry

    D.   moiety

IV.   Recognize the major systems of kinship terminology:

    A.   Eskimo

    B.   Hawaiian

    C.   Iroquois

    D.   Crow

Key Terms and Names

ambilineal descent
clan
Crow system
descent group
double descent
Eskimo system
fission
Hawaiian system
Iroquois system
Kindred

kinship
Lewis Henry Morgan
lineage
matrilineal descent
moiety
patrilineal descent
phratry
totemism
unilineal descent

Exercises

1. On the two charts provided below, color in a *matrilineal descent group* and a *patrilineal descent group*.

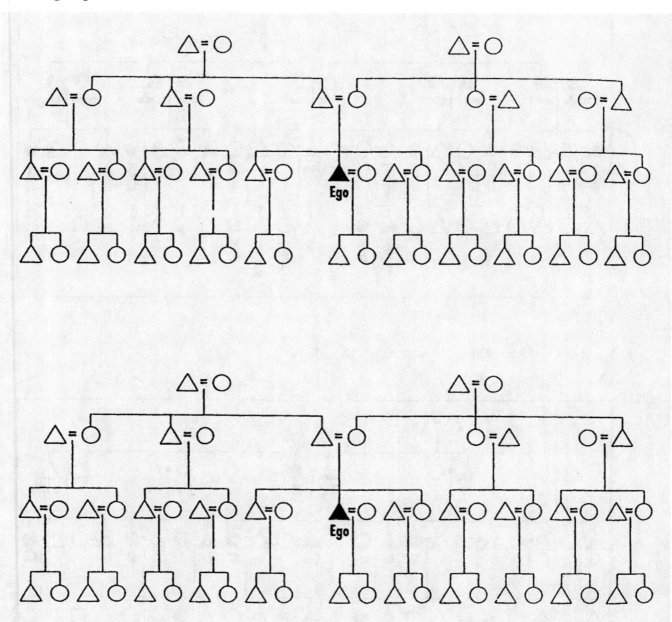

2. What kind of terminological system is shown here?

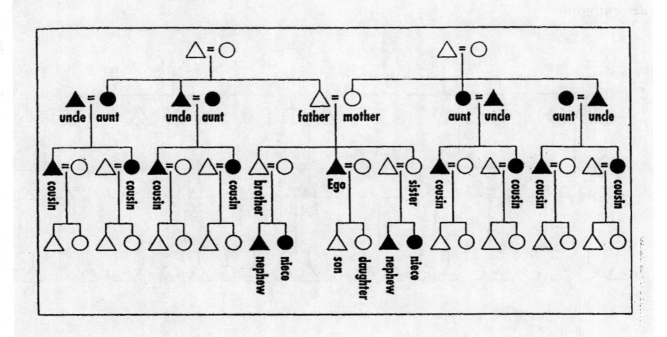

3. What kind of terminological system is shown here?

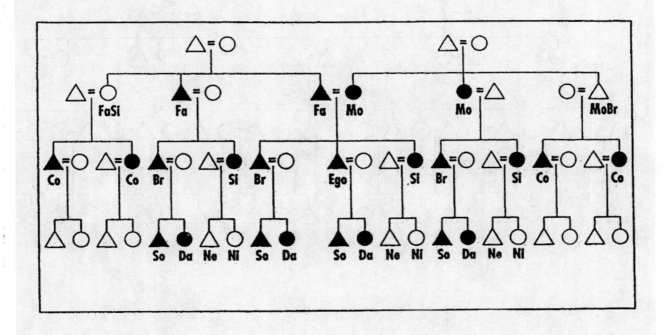

4. What kind of terminological system is shown here?

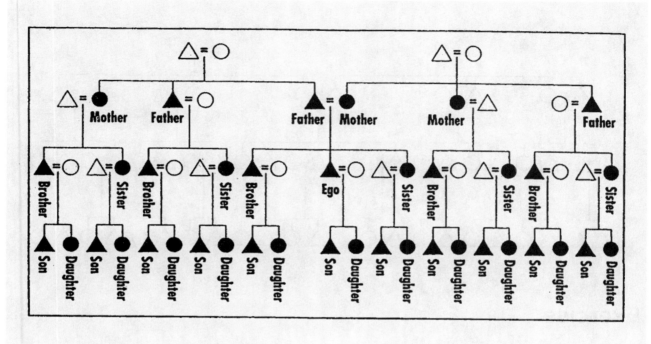

5. In the system below, what should Ego call the individual marked "X"?

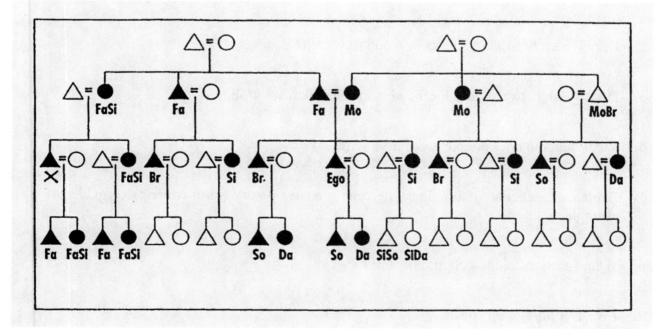

6. On the chart below, illustrate a descriptive type terminological system.

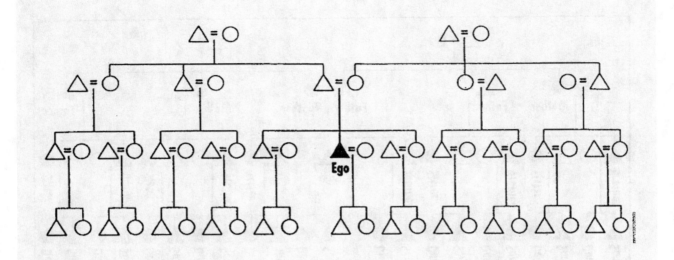

Exercise

Review Questions

1. Why do societies form descent groups?

2. How is membership in a descent group restricted?

3. Distinguish between patrilineal and matrilineal descent groups

4. What function does double descent serve in Yako society?

5. Explain the function of ambilineal descent in contemporary North America. Provide an example.

6. What functions do descent groups serve?

7. How is a lineage reckoned?

8. What are the social implications of lineage exogamy?

9. Contrast a clan and a lineage.

10. What did anthropologist Magery Wolf find out about the situation of women in Taiwan?

11. What purpose do totems serve a clan?

12. Distinguish between a phratry and a moiety.

13. How do bilateral systems differ from unilateral systems?

14. What are the functions and limitations of ego-centered groups?

15. Why do descent groups emerge?

16. What functions do kinship terminologies serve?

17. What are the six major systems of kinship terminology?

18. What is the main feature of the Eskimo system of descent?

19. What is the simplest descent system? Why is it considered simple?

20. With which type of descent group is Iroquois terminology commonly correlated?

21. How can anthropologists assist Native Americans in their struggles for federal recognition?

Multiple-Choice Practice Questions

1. Descent groups _____.
   a. are composed of those who claim to be lineally descended from a particular ancestor
   b. are common in human societies
   c. trace their connections back to a common ancestor through a chain of parent-child links, and thus appear to stem from the parent-child bond
   d. help provide jobs for their members
   e. "are composed of those who claim to be lineally descended from a particular ancestor", "are common in human societies" and "trace their connections back to a common ancestor through a chain of parent-child links, and thus appear to stem from the parent-child bond"

2. By tracing membership either through males or through females, members of unilineal descent groups _____.
   a. know exactly to which group they belong and where their primary loyalties lie
   b. are confused about their relationship to persons not included in the group
   c. act like females if they are in a matrilineal group
   d. act life males if they are in a patrilineal group
   e. know exactly how many children they are going to have

3. You belong to a patrilineal descent group. Which of the following belong to the same group?
   a. your mother
   b. your father's sister
   c. your mother's sister
   d. your mother's father
   e. your father's sister's children

4. The primary way in which a woman in traditional China could exert any influence was _____.
   a. through her close tie with her husband
   b. by appealing to her mother-in-law who will intercede with her husband on her behalf
   c. by threatening to return to her own people
   d. through the influence of her brothers
   e. through the village women's gossip which can cause a loss of face for her husband and father-in-law

5. A boy is born into a society that practices matrilineal descent. The person who exercises authority over him is _____.
   a. his sister
   b. his father
   c. his mother
   d. his mother's brother
   e. his father's sister

6. Among the Yako of Nigeria, an individual might inherit grazing lands from his father's patrilineal group, and livestock and ritual knowledge from his mother's matrilineal group. This is an example of _____ descent.
   a. ambilineal
   b. bilocal
   c. patrilateral
   d. indivisible
   e. double

7. A cousins club _____.
   a. is an ambilineal descent group to which younger-generation descendants of east European Jewish immigrants belong
   b. is a double descent group to which only cross cousins belong
   c. is a patrilineal descent group composed of the children of Norman Cousins
   d. is a cognatic descent group composed of women only
   e. is a unlineal descent group for first and second cousins

8. Descent groups _____.
   a. are economic units providing mutual aid
   b. provide social security for elderly members
   c. often promote solidarity by encouraging worship of the group's ancestors
   d. play a role in deciding appropriate marriage partners
   e. "are economic units providing mutual aid", "provide social security for elderly members", "often promote solidarity by encouraging worship of the group's ancestors" and "play a role in deciding appropriate marriage partners"

9. A lineage is a corporate descent group _____.
   a. the members of which can buy shares in the corporation
   b. the members of which claim descent from a common ancestor
   c. the members of which know the exact genealogical linkages by which they are related to the common ancestor
   d. composed of consanguineal kin
   e. "the members of which claim descent from a common ancestor", "the members of which know the exact genealogical linkages by which they are related to the common ancestor" and "composed of consanguineal kin"

10. A totem _____.

    a. is a word that comes from the Ojibwa American Indian word that means "he is a relative of mine."

    b. is a symbol of animals, plants, natural forces, and objects

    c. is usually associated with a clan's concept of its mythical origins

    d. may be found in our own society in the names we give to baseball and football teams

    e. "is a word that comes from the Ojibwa American Indian word that means 'he is a relative of mine.'", "is a symbol of animals, plants, natural forces, and objects", "is usually associated with a clan's concept of its mythical origins" and "may be found in our own society in the names we give to baseball and football teams"

11. A phratry is a unilineal descent group composed of two or more _____ that believe they are related to each other.

    a. moieties

    b. totems

    c. kindred

    d. lineages

    e. clans

12. Members of a moiety _____.

    a. belong to one of two major descent groups in a society

    b. are those who are divorced (they lack their "better half")

    c. are usually able to trace their exact genealogical links to their common ancestor

    d. feel a much stronger feeling of kinship than is felt by members of a lineage or clan

    e. belong to a group that is smaller than a lineage

13. A person in a system of bilateral descent _____.

    a. traces descent through the father for some purposes and through the mother for other purposes

    b. traces descent through female lines

    c. traces descent through male lines

    d. uses totems to symbolically represent the group

    e. traces descent through both parents simultaneously and recognizes multiple ancestors

14. Descent groups are frequently found to be important organizing devices in _____.

    a. food-foraging societies

    b. horticultural societies

    c. pastoral societies

    d. intensive agricultural societies

    e. horticultural societies, pastoral societies and intensive agricultural societies

15. _____ develop out of extended families when families split up and move to nearby regions, and the core members of these families recognize their descent from a common ancestor and continue to organize activities based on this idea.
    a. Phratries
    b. Kindred groups
    c. Lineages
    d. Moieties
    e. Cognatic groups

16. If two people are given the same kinship term, this means that _____.
    a. they have the same genes
    b. no one can tell the difference between them
    c. they occupy a similar status
    d. they are identical twins
    e. they are members of an adopted family

17. In _____ kinship terminology, ego's "brother" and "sister" are distinguished from "cousins"; both ego's father's brother and mother's brother are given the same kinship term, "uncle."
    a. Eskimo
    b. Hawaiian
    c. Crow
    d. Omaha
    e. Iroquois

18. In the _____ system of kinship terminology, ego's father, father's brother, and mother's brother are all referred to by the same term, and ego's mother, mother's sister, and father's sister are all referred to by the same term; the term "brother" includes ego's brothers as well as male cousins.
    a. Iroquois
    b. Crow
    c. Omaha
    d. Hawaiian
    e. Eskimo

19. In _____ kinship terminology, the term "brother" is given to ego's brother, father's brother's son, and mother's sister's son; a different term is used for the sons of father's sister and mother's brother. "Mother" refers to ego's mother and mother's sister; "father" refers to ego's father and father's brother. Separate terms are used for ego's mother's brother and father's sister.
    a. Eskimo
    b. Hawaiian
    c. Iroquois
    d. cognatic
    e. kindred

20. The Crow kinship terminology system _____.
    a.   is associated with matrilineal descent
    b.   merges paternal cross-cousins with the paternal generation
    c.   is associated with patrilineal descent
    d.   merges maternal cross-cousins with the generation of ego's children
    e.   "is associated with matrilineal descent", "merges paternal cross-cousins with the paternal generation" and "merges maternal cross-cousins with the generation of ego's children"

21. The Omaha kinship terminology system _____.
    a.   is associated with partrilineal descent
    b.   merges maternal cross-cousins with the parental generation
    c.   merges paternal cross-cousins with the generation of ego's children
    d.   identifies maternal cross-cousins with the lineage of ego's mother (the lineage that supplies women to ego's patrilineage)
    e.   "is associated with partrilineal descent", "merges maternal cross-cousins with the parental generation", "merges paternal cross-cousins with the generation of ego's children" and "identifies maternal cross-cousins with the lineage of ego's mother (the lineage that supplies women to ego's patrilineage)"

22. Which of the following would **not** be considered typical activities outside the house of a rural Taiwanese woman?
    a.   wash clothes on the riverbank
    b.   clean and pare vegetables at a communal pump
    c.   mend clothes under a tree
    d.   stop to rest on a bench with other women
    e.   shop at the market place

23. In autumn 1981, Dutch anthropologist _____ went to Maine to check out a job at the Association of Aroostook Indians, which needed a research and development director.
    a.   Lewis Henry Morgan
    b.   Fred Plog
    c.   G.P. Murdock
    d.   Weston LaBarre
    e.   Harald Prins

24. This major theoretician of nineteenth-century North American anthropology has been regarded as the founder of kinship studies.
    a.   Margaret Mead
    b.   Leslie White
    c.   Julian Steward
    d.   Lewis Henry Morgan
    e.   Geoffrey Gorer

25. The production of the world's first "test-tube" baby, in a petri dish outside the womb, without sexual intercourse took place in what year?

    a. 1978

    b. 1965

    c. 1954

    d. 1988

    e. 1995

26. All societies have found some form of family and/or household organization a convenient way to deal with problems all human groups encounter. Which of the following would be problems all human groups face?

    a. how to facilitate economic cooperation between the sexes

    b. when to retire

    c. how to regulate sexual activity

    d. how to provide a proper setting for child rearing

    e. "how to facilitate economic cooperation between the sexes", "how to regulate sexual activity" and "how to provide a proper setting for child rearing"

27. Important though family membership was for each individual in the traditional Chinese patrilineal society, it was the _____ that was regarded as the primary social unit.

    a. nuclear family

    b. extended family

    c. *tsu*

    d. *mu shoo*

    e. *chow su bao*

28. Two or more clans together constitute larger units called _____.

    a. moieties

    b. phratries

    c. extended families

    d. blended families

    e. ambilocal clans

29. The descent system that allows each individual the option of affiliating with either the mother's or the father's descent group is known as _____ descent.

    a. double

    b. matrilineal

    c. patrilineal

    d. avunculocal

    e. ambilineal

30. In the years prior to World War II younger-generation descendants of east European Jewish immigrants sought to separate themselves from older generations while still maintaining the traditional Jewish ethic of family solidarity formed what has come to be known as _____.

    a. family circles

    b. private clubs

    c. cousin clubs

    d. gangs

    e. fraternities

31. The _____, like Microsoft and Intel, is a corporate group.

    a. lineage

    b. clan

    c. clique

    d. cousin club

    e. fraternity

32. In some cultures, lineages facing exceptional challenges to their survival may choose to ritually adopt individuals not related by birth. Such was the case among the _____ in the 17th and 18th centuries.

    a. Apache

    b. Iroquois

    c. Lakota

    d. Chumash

    e. Onandaga

33. The kin-ordered social structure of the Winnebago Indian nation offers an interesting ethnographic example of a _____ system.

    a. lineage

    b. clan

    c. phratry

    d. moiety

    e. ambilocal

34. Which of the following systems of kinship terminology was **not** discussed in your textbook?

    a. Crow

    b. Iroquois

    c. Hawaiian

    d. Kariera

    e. Eskimo

35. Patriclans trace descent exclusively through men from a founding ancestor. Historically, a few dozen of such clans existed in the _____.
    a. Torey Islands.
    b. Guatemalan Highlands.
    c. Canadian provinces.
    d. Australian Outback
    e. Scottish Highlands.

True/False Practice Questions

1. Cross-cousins are ideal marriage partners in an arrangement whereby lineages engage in reciprocal marriage exchanges to establish alliances.
   True or False

2. Omaha kinship terminology is the matrilineal equivalent of the Crow system.
   True or False

3. The kindred is a kin group that is organized laterally rather than lineally.
   True or False

4. The boundaries of a kindred are permanent and definite.
   True or False

5. Women in rural Taiwan live their lives in the walled courtyards of their husbands' households.
   True or False

6. It is in their relations in the outside world that women develop sufficient backing to maintain some independence under their powerful mothers-in-law.
   True or False

7. The shy young Taiwanese girl who enters the village as a bride is examined as frankly and suspiciously by the women as an animal that is up for sale.
   True or False

8. A Taiwanese girl who gossips freely about the affairs of her husband's household may find herself always on the outside of the group, or worse yet, accused of snobbery.
   True or False

9. In rural Taiwan women can serve as a powerful protective force for their defenseless younger members, in this way they are a very liberated force in the village.
   True or False

10. Even older rural Taiwanese women who have raised their sons properly retain little influence over their sons' actions, especially in activities exclusive to men.
    True or False

11. A Taiwanese woman is subject to an important set of rules, and to be successful she must strictly obey those rules.
    True or False

12. A truly successful Taiwanese woman is a rugged individualist who has learned to depend largely on herself while appearing to lean on the males in her family.
True or False

13. Unilineal descent provides an easy way of restricting descent group membership so as to minimize problems of divided loyalty and the like.
True or False

14. Bilateral kinship and bilateral descent cannot be used interchangeably since they different meanings.
True or False

15. Descent groups don't need to clearly define membership to operate efficiently.
True or False

16. In a society where descent is traced patrilineally, maternal relatives are less important.
True or False

17. Double descent, whereby descent is reckoned both patrilineally and matrilineally at the same time, is very rare.
True or False

18. Because of its bilateral structure, a kindred is never the same for any two persons except siblings. Thus, no two people (except siblings) belong to the same kindred.
True or False

19. Each Scottish clan has its own traditional tartan, the patterns themselves are extremely ancient.
True or False

20. The traditional Scottish tartans are a colorful symbol of a shared heritage between even very distant relatives living very far apart.
True or False

21. It is now possible for a woman to give birth to her genetic uncle.
True or False

Practice Short Answer Questions

1. Describe the kin-ordered social structure of the Winnebago Indian nation.

2. Explain why Scottish clans continue to survive.

3. What is meant by "new reproductive techniques (NRT)?"

4. Due to "new reproductive techniques (NRT)," it has been suggested that at least ten different terms are needed to cover the concepts of "mother" and "father" in Western societies. Identify those suggested terms.

Practice Essays

1. Compare and contrast the social organization of the Hopi and the Chinese.

2. Many North American feminists are interested in the concept of matriarchy, sometimes confusing it with or linking it to the matrilineal descent system. Does matrilineality imply matriarchy? Use concrete examples to explore this.

3. Describe a typical woman's life in rural Taiwan from the time she enters her husband's family as a new bride to the time she reaches seniority in his household as a mother-in-law.

4. Describe how women in patrilineal societies like Taiwan actively manipulate the system to their own advantage as best they can.

5. Identify at least ten different terms that are needed to cover the concepts of "mother" and "father' in Western societies.

6. Discuss the inevitable changes that will have to occur with traditional notions of kinship and gender, due to the advent of new reproductive technologies that separate conception from birth and eggs from wombs.

7. Descent groups are convenient devices for solving a number of problems human societies commonly confront. Identify the problems and describe how a descent group solves them.

8. Discuss the forms and functions of descent groups.

9. The culture's descent system is closely tied to a society's economic base. Explain why this is so.

Solutions

Multiple-Choice Practice Questions

1. E
2. A
3. B
4. E
5. D
6. E
7. A
8. E
9. E
10. E
11. E
12. A
13. E
14. E
15. C
16. C
17. A
18. D
19. C
20. E
21. E
22. E
23. E
24. D
25. A
26. E
27. C
28. B
29. E
30. C
31. A
32. B
33. D
34. D
35. E

True/False Practice Questions

1. T
2. F
3. T
4. F
5. F
6. T
7. T
8. T
9. F
10. F
11. F
12. T
13. T
14. T
15. F
16. F
17. T
18. T
19. F
20. T
21. T

Chapter 11

Grouping by Gender, Age, Common Interest, and Class

Synopsis

Chapter 11 examines major kinds of nonkin organizations. Groups defined by gender, age, and common interest are described. Finally, stratified forms of social organization such as those involving class or caste are presented.

What You Should Learn from This Chapter

I.   Understand the functions of nonkin groupings:

    A.   sex

    B.   age

    C.   common interests

II.   Know how societies are stratified and the reasons for social divisions.

III.   Understand the differences between class and caste-type stratification.

Key Terms

age grade

age set

caste

closed-class societies

common-interest association

egalitarian society

mobility

open-class societies

social class

stratified society

symbolic indicators

verbal evaluation

Exercise

Briefly identify and locate the following cultures.

1. Iroquois

2. South African

3. Tiriki

4. Maya

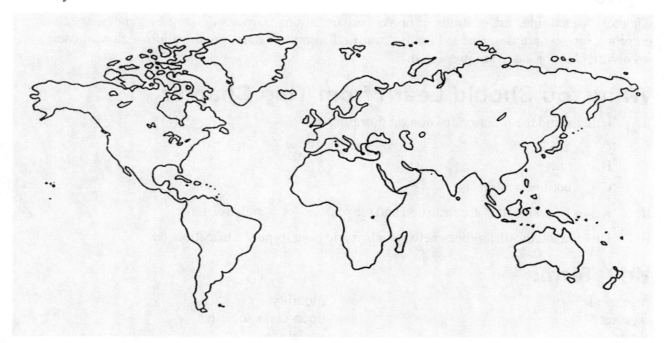

Exercise

Review Questions

1. Describe the separate but equal organization of the Iroquois.

2. In what ways is age grouping evidenced in North America?

3. How does one become a member of an age grade?

4. Distinguish between an age group and an age set.

5. Describe the Tiriki age-set system.

6. How and why are common-interest associations formed?

7. Historically, why have women's groups been less common than men's?

8. What functions do women's associations have?

9. What purposes do urban-oriented associations serve?

10. Describe the interstrata relationship in a stratified society.

11. Contrast an egalitarian society with a stratified society.

12. In what ways might a society be stratified?

13. Briefly describe India's caste system.

14. How might a stratified society beget an outcast group?

15. What are three aspects of a social-class structure?

16. Distinguish between the three ways social class are manifest in society.

17. What is social-impact assessment?

18. What role does religion play in India's caste system?

19. How and why did the Maya develop a stratified society?

20. What are "virtual" common-interest associations?

Fill-in-the-Blank

1. An age _____ is a category based on age, a stage through which people pass (such as a "teenager").

2. An age _____ is a group of people who move through life stages together (such as "baby boomers").

3. Among the _____ of South America, men and women work, eat, and sleep separately.

4. Common-interest associations used to be called _____ associations.

5. The text suggests that the caste system is present not only in India but also in _____ , _____ and _____ .

6. A _____ society is one in which members do not share equally in prestige and basic resources.

7. _____ is a special form of social class in which membership is determined by birth and remains fixed for life.

8. In a class society, people are theoretically able to change their class positions through social _____ .

Multiple-Choice Practice Questions

1. High rates of rape appear to be associated with societies in which the roles of males and females are highly segregated, and in which there are efforts by males to be dominant over women. If this is true, we would expect the highest rate of rape to occur among the _____.
   a. Ju/'hoansi
   b. Mundurucu
   c. Iroquois
   d. Mbuti
   e. Hopi

2. In literate societies that rely on the written word for accumulated wisdom, elders are often _____.
   a. treated with great respect because of their wisdom
   b. considered to be as valuable as their weight in gold
   c. treated like "living libraries" that contain much needed knowledge
   d. not considered sources of information
   e. killed when they turn sixty-five years old

3. The following _____ are passed through by members of North American culture: toddler, teenager, senior citizen.
   a. age grades
   b. age sets
   c. social classes
   d. castes
   e. open classes

4. Which of the following statements about common-interest associations is **incorrect**?
   a. They were originally referred to in the anthropological literature as voluntary associations
   b. Common-interest associations are more common in hunter-gatherer societies than in urban-industrial societies
   c. Common-interest associations are intimately associated with world urbanization and increasing social complexity
   d. Common-interest associations are found in many traditional societies
   e. Sometimes one can join a common-interest association voluntarily, and sometimes membership is required by law

5. The text suggests that women's participation in common-interest associations in traditional societies is often less than men's because _____.
   a. women are less sociable than men
   b. women have no interests in common because they see each other as sexual competitors
   c. women remain at home, isolated from other women
   d. men prevent women from joining such groupings
   e. women have so many opportunities to socialize that they have little need for common-interest associations.

6. In times of rapid social change _____.
   a. common-interest associations decline in significance
   b. common-interest associations assume the roles and functions formerly held by kinship or age groups
   c. women form common-interest associations whereas men retain their membership in age and kinship groups
   d. men are able to adapt whereas women are not
   e. the role of the elderly becomes more important as the society adjusts to change

7. A society composed of several groups that differ in their access to resources and prestige is said to be _____.
   a. stratified
   b. unfair
   c. immoral
   d. egalitarian
   e. open

8. A/An _____ is a special form of social class in which membership is determined by birth and remains fixed for life.

    a. clan
    b. phratry
    c. common-interest association
    d. age group
    e. caste

9. Symbolic indicators may not always be reliable in helping you assess someone's class status. Which of the following is an example of this?

    a. A common form of recreation of lower-class males is playing pool at the local beer joint
    b. A con man from a lower-class background wears a tuxedo when he tries to sell you shares in a nonexistent corporation
    c. According to Emily Post, one can always identify upper-crust families by the presence of a day maid
    d. Demille O'Hara, striving to return to the simplicity of life as lived by his tribal ancestors, lets his day maid go
    e. A con man from a lower-class background wears a tuxedo when he "tries to sell you shares in a nonexistent corporation", "Demille O'Hara, striving to return to the simplicity of life as lived by his tribal ancestors, lets his day maid go"

10. The ability to change one's class position is known as _____.

    a. open class
    b. egalitarian
    c. social mobility
    d. indicative of common-interest societies
    e. inevitable

11. The degree of social mobility in a stratified society is related to _____.

    a. the prevailing kind of family organization
    b. its ideology
    c. the number of different common-interest associations it has
    d. the difference between its richest and poorest classes
    e. genetic factors

12. Which of the following could have contributed to the emergence of social stratification?

    a. All human beings want to be looked up to by their fellow members of society

    b. Certain descent groups may have monopolized activities that turned out to play an important role in their society (such as propitiation of the gods in a horticultural society exposed to unpredictable weather)

    c. An ethnic group with an economic or military advantage (such as knowledge of intensive agriculture or possession of firearms) that enters a foreign territory may become the ruling class within that area

    d. "All human beings want to be looked up to by their fellow members of society", "Certain descent groups may have monopolized activities that turned out to play an important role in their society (such as propitiation of the gods in a horticultural society exposed to unpredictable weather)" and "An ethnic group with an economic or military advantage (such as knowledge of intensive agriculture or possession of firearms) that enters a foreign territory may become the ruling class within that area"

    e. none of these

13. A kind of policy research frequently done by an anthropologist is called a _____.

    a. ethnology

    b. ethnography

    c. participant observation

    d. social impact assessment

    e. need assessment

14. In the U.S., any project requiring a federal permit or licence, or using federal funds, by law must be preceded by a _____.

    a. need assessment

    b. archaeological assessment

    c. cultural impact assessment

    d. assessment of feasibility

    e. social impact statement

15. Anthropologist _____ was hired to carry out a social impact assessment of a water diversion project in New Mexico.

    a. Sue Ellen Jacobs

    b. Harald Prins

    c. R.M. Bradfield

    d. P.R. Sanday

    e. Fred Plog

16. What the term _____ really refers to are those associations not based on sex, age, kinship, marriage, or territory that result from an act of joining.

    a. clan

    b. age grade

    c. voluntary association

    d. neighborhood association

    e. womens' auxiliary

17. Which of the following is not an example of a common-interest organization?

    a. the American Federation of Labor

    b. the National Rifle Association

    c. the Navajo Nation

    d. the Aryan Nation

    e. the Green Party

18. Which of the following would be reasons for the decline in membership in common-interest associations in the United States?

    a. viewing television

    b. frequent moves

    c. long working hours

    d. the Internet

    e. viewing television, frequent moves, long working hours and the Internet

19. Social scientists have observed that today, with outright unemployment at historically low levels, the _____ provides a pool of cheap labor.

    a. lower castes

    b. middle-class

    c. underclass

    d. mentally-challenged

    e. pariah groups

20. In which of the following societies are men and women rigidly segregated in what they do?

    a. Seneca

    b. Oneida

    c. Mohawk

    d. Onondaga

    e. Seneca, Oneida, Mohawk and Onondaga

21. Age grouping is so familiar and so important that it and _____ sometimes have been called the only universal factors for determining a person's position in society.
    a. height
    b. weight
    c. eye color
    d. sex
    e. shoe size

22. The members of a/an _____ usually remain closely associated throughout their lives, or at least most of their lives.
    a. fraternity
    b. sorority
    c. union
    d. kindred
    e. age set

23. All stratified societies offer at least some _____, and this helps to ease the strains in any system of inequality.
    a. stability
    b. reliability
    c. instability
    d. mobility
    e. shakiness

24. In which of the following ways are societies stratified?
    a. gender
    b. age
    c. social class
    d. caste
    e. gender, age, social class and caste

25. The highest caste in the Indian system is the _____ caste.
    a. Harijan
    b. Brahmans
    c. Vaisyas
    d. Shudras
    e. Kshatriyas

26. The fighters and rulers in the Indian system come from the _____ caste.
    a. Shudras
    b. Harijan
    c. Vaisyas
    d. Brahman
    e. Kshatriyas

27. In the Indian system, those members of the Vaisyas caste are the _____.
    a. fighters and rulers.
    b. merchants and traders.
    c. artisans and laborers.
    d. "untouchables."
    e. priests and lawgivers.

28. The artists and laborers are members of the _____caste in the Indian system.
    a. Shudras
    b. Harijan
    c. Vaisyas
    d. Brahmans
    e. Kshatriyas

29. In which of the following countries might a caste-like system be found?
    a. Canada
    b. France
    c. Italy
    d. Bolivia
    e. Argentina

30. A caste-like system based on skin color and wealth once existed in _____ where a white minority created a political regime Apartheid.
    a. Germany
    b. Holland
    c. Belgium
    d. Sudan
    e. South Africa

31. The director of the African Burial Ground Project was biological anthropologist _____.
    a. Jennifer Thompson.
    b. Victoria Cassman
    c. Sheila Brooks
    d. Michael Blakey
    e. Summer Decker

True/False Practice Questions

1. Division of labor by sex is characteristic of all human societies.
   True or False

2. Usually an increase in the number of common-interest associations is associated with urbanization, but these associations are also found in traditional societies.
   True or False

3. Castes are strongly exogamous.
    True or False

4. Mobility refers to the ability to change one's class position.
    True or False

5. An age grade is a group of people initiated into the group at the same time who move though the series of categories together.
    True or False

6. One of the major objections to the construction of the water diversion project in New Mexico is that it would result in the obliteration of the three-hundred-year-old irrigation system structures.
    True or False

7. Observers have noted a recent decrease in participation in all sorts of common-interest associations.
    True or False

8. According to Mundurucu beliefs men have always ruled over women.
    True or False

9. Like age grades, age sets cease to exist after a specified number of years.
    True or False

10. Common-interest associations have proliferated modern society, but are not found in many traditional societies.
    True or False

11. The Indian caste system has absolutely no flexibility and/or mobility.
    True or False

12. A caste-like system could never have existed in the United States.
    True or False

13. Individuals born and raised within large-scale societies face the challenge of succeeding within a complex social structure that extends well beyond kinship.
    True or False

14. India's national constitution of 1950 abolished caste discrimination and the practice of untouchability, in effect doing away with the caste system.
    True or False

Practice Matching

Match the culture with its characteristic.

1. _____ Iroquois
2. _____ Tiriki
3. _____ South Africans
4. _____ Maya
5. _____ Apsarok (Crow) Indians

a. African nomadic pastoralists with an age set/age grade system.
b. Castelike social organization based on racial divisions.
c. Native Americans with separate but equal gender organization.
d. Stratified society of pre-Columbian Central America.
e. Women were allowed to participate in the secret Tobacco Society.

Practice Short Answer Questions

1. Discuss India's untouchables and their plight.

2. What is the "one drop" rule?

3. Under what conditions does social stratification become a problem?

Practice Essays

1. Marx felt that religion was "the opiate of the masses," claiming that it was often used by the upper classes to perpetuate their own dominance. Can this perspective be applied to the Indian caste system? Would it be ethnocentric to do so?

2. What were the findings of the social impact assessment of the water diversion project in New Mexico?

3. Although important differences exist, there are nonetheless interesting similarities between Mundurucu beliefs and those of traditional European culture. Discuss those similarities.

4. Compare and contrast stratified societies with egalitarian societies.

5. Some observers have noted a recent decline in participation in all types of common-interest organizations, at least in North America. What is the explanation for this decline? Explain.

6.   The classic ethnographic example of a caste system is the Hindu caste system of India. Describe that system.

7.   Discuss the caste-like social system called Apartheid that was established in South Africa.

8.   Describe how social classes make life oppressive for large numbers of people, while at the same time performing an integrative function in society.

9.   What were the findings of the African Burial Ground Project?

Solutions

Fill-in-the-Blank

1. grade

2. set

3. Mundurucu

4. voluntary

5. South Africa, the U.S., China

6. stratified

7. A caste

8. mobility

Multiple-Choice Practice Questions

1. B

2. D

3. A

4. B

5. E

6. B

7. A

8. E

9. E

10. C

11. A

12. D

13. D

14. E

15. A

16. C

17. C

18. E

19. C

20. E

21. D

22. E

23. D

24. E

25. B

26. E

27. B

28. A

29. D

30. E

31. D

True/False Practice Questions

1. T

2. T

3. F

4. T

5. F

6. T

7. T

8. F

9. F

10. F

11. F

12. F

13. T

14. F

Practice Matching

1. C

2. A

3. B

4. D

5. E

Chapter 12

Politics, Power, and Violence

Synopsis

Chapter 12 defines politics as a system that maintains social order within and between societies. Decentralized and centralized type of political systems are described and an attempt is made to define "law" in cross-cultural terms. The concepts of authority and legitimacy are discussed and various kinds of leadership are examined.

What You Should Learn from This Chapter

I. Know the four major kinds of political organization:

    A.   bands

    B.   tribes

    C.   chiefdoms

    D.   states

II.   Understand how internal political and social control is maintained in different political systems.

III.   Understand how external affairs are conducted in different political systems.

IV.   Understand how conflicts are resolved and the functions of law.

V.   Recognize the impact of religion on social control.

Key Terms

adjudication

band

chiefdom

cultural control

law

legitimacy

mediation

nation

negotiation

sanctions

segmentary lineage system

social control

state

tribe

world view

Exercises

1. Fill in the chart below, giving examples of each of the major types of political systems and describing their general characteristics. You can use this to study from later.

TYPES OF POLITICAL SYSTEMS		
Type	Example	Characteristics
Band		
Tribe		
Chiefdom		
State		

2. Briefly identify and locate the following cultures.
A. Nuer
B. Kpelle
C. Igbo
D. Bedouin
E. Abenaki
F. Swazi

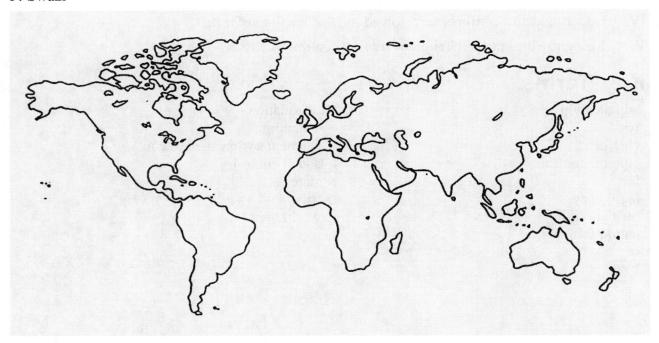

Exercise

Review Questions

1. What are the four basic kinds of political systems?

2. What kinds of societies typically have uncentralized systems?

3. How is authority conferred in a band?

4. How is authority conferred in a tribe?

5. Distinguish between the segmentary lineage system and the clan.

6. What is the role of the leopard-skin chief of the Nuer?

7. What is the function of age-grade systems in the political structure of tribes?

8. Describe the role of the *tonowi* among the Kapauku Papuans.

9. What kinds of societies typically have centralized political systems?

10. Distinguish between nation and state.

11. What has women's role generally been in political leadership?

12. Describe women's role in Igbo society.

13. How is social control generally maintained in bands and tribes?

14. How do internalized controls guide behavior?

15. Distinguish between positive and negative sanctions.

16. Distinguish between informal and formal sanctions.

17. What are the limits on power in Bedouin society?

18. Why is the definition of law destined to be inexact?

19. What are the functions of law?

20. Differentiate between negotiation, adjudication, and mediation.

21. How are disputes handled by the Kpelle?

22. Why might warfare be so prominent in food-producing societies?

23. Compare the world view of the Abenaki with that of the Iroquois.

24. Distinguish between force and legitimacy.

25. In what ways is religion connected with politics?

26. What does the term *political organization* refer to?

27. Identify three groups of people, and the area where they live, who do not practice warfare as we know it.

Fill-in-the-Blank

1. The term _____ refers to the system of social relationships that is connected with the maintenance of public order.

2. The term _____ refers to an administrative system having specialized personnel.

3. Anthropologists have identified four types of political systems; two are said to be _____ and two _____ .

4. An egalitarian, autonomous small group composed of related people who occupy a single region is called a _____ .

5. All humans were food foragers living in band-type organizations until about _____ years ago.

6. The _____ are an example of a society practicing band-level organization.

7. Most conflict in bands is settled by informal means, and decisions are usually made by _____ .

8. A _____ is a larger grouping than a band and is linked to a specific territory.

9. A form of political organization in which a larger group is broken up into clans that are then divided into lineages, is called a _____ lineage system.

10. Among the Nuer, the tendency for widespread feuding to occur among lineages is counterbalanced by the actions of the _____ .

11. In tribal societies of Melanesia, a type of leader called the _____ or *tonowi* is prevalent.

12. A _____ is a ranked society in which every member has a position in the hierarchy.

13. Chiefdoms are linked to _____ economic systems.

14. The Swazi have a _____ -level political system.

15. States are typically linked to _____ subsistence patterns.

16. An example of a society in which women play a notably strong political role is the _____ .

17. The Wape of New Guinea use belief in _____ as a means of social control.

18. In North America we rely on both external and _____ controls to maintain social order.

19. Among the Bedouin _____ sanctions restrict the inappropriate use of power by those in authority.

20. The Inuit use _____ as a means of resolving conflict.

21. Malinowski distinguished law from _____ by whether there was a "definite social machinery of binding force."

22. Western societies make a distinction between _____ law, involving offenses committed against individuals, and _____ law, involving offenses committed against the state.

23. Disputes may be settled by _____ , the use of direct argument and compromise by the disputing parties, or by _____ , settlement through the assistance of an unbiased third party.

24. Warfare is most closely linked to the _____ -type political system.

Multiple-Choice Practice Questions

1. The term "government" may be defined as _____.

    a. a kinship-based age set

    b. those aspects of social organization concerned with coordination and regulation of public behavior

    c. the informal leadership of a Ju/'hoansi hunter-gatherer band

    d. common-interest association focusing on political events

    e. an administrative system having specialized personnel

2. Bands and tribes are both _____.

    a. centralized

    b. associated with industrialism

    c. dependent on age groups for political organization

    d. uncentralized and egalitarian

    e. hierarchical in social organization

3. The form of social organization typical of hunter-gatherers is the _____, whereas horticulture and pastoralism are usually associated with the form of social organization called the _____.

    a. tribe/chiefdom

    b. tribe/state

    c. tribe/band

    d. band/chiefdom

    e. band/tribe

4. The "leopard-skin chief" among the Nuer _____.

    a. is the head of the largest and most powerful clan

    b. is the head of the dominant matrilineage

    c. has the authority to force feuding lineages to accept "blood cattle" and stop feuding

    d. tries to mediate between feuding sides but does not have political power

    e. is the totem of one of the Nuer lineages

5. Age-grade systems and common-interest associations are effective methods of integrating small autonomous units such as bands into larger social units. These methods may be described as _____ systems of political organization.

    a. segmentary

    b. negotiated

    c. state

    d. nonkinship

    e. kinship

6. A _____ is a ranked society in which every member has a position in the hierarchy, and an individual's status is determined by membership in a descent group.
    a. band
    b. tribe
    c. chiefdom
    d. state
    e. kindred

7. The state is distinctive in the extensiveness of its legitimate use of _____ to regulate the affairs of its citizens.
    a. kinship
    b. force
    c. chiefs
    d. religion
    e. gossip

8. In a chiefdom, an individual's status is determined by membership in a _____.
    a. government
    b. social class
    c. bureaucracy
    d. descent group
    e. secret society

9. A cross-cultural comparison of systems of political organization reveals that _____.
    a. many women who hold high office do so by virtue of their relationship to men
    b. many women in positions of leadership adopt characteristics of temperament that are usually considered masculine
    c. in a number of societies, women have as much political power as men
    d. women may play an important role in political decisions even when they are not visible public leaders
    e. "many women who hold high office do so by virtue of their relationship to men", "many women in positions of leadership adopt characteristics of temperament that are usually considered masculine", "in a number of societies, women have as much political power as men" and "women may play an important role in political decisions even when they are not visible public leaders"

10. At he heart of political organization is _____.
    a. control of unacceptable social behavior
    b. the legitimate use of force to maintain order
    c. unequal access to power
    d. the dominance of males over females
    e. the development of egalitarian relationships

11. Sanctions refer to _____.
    a. internalized social controls
    b. holy behavior
    c. externalized social controls
    d. decadent behavior
    e. ritualized behavior

12. _____ sanctions attempt to precisely and explicitly regulate people's behavior. They can be positive (such as military decorations) or negative (such as imprisonment).
    a. Hierarchical
    b. Egalitarian
    c. Informal
    d. Formal
    e. Magical

13. In centralized societies, antisocial behavior is usually dealt with in a court system by the use of formal, negative sanctions involving the application of abstract rules and the use of force. The primary aim is _____.
    a. to help the victim
    b. to renew social relations between the victim and the perpetrator of the crime
    c. to prevent witchcraft from being used
    d. to assign and punish guilt
    e. to provide a good show for the spectators

14. The functions of law include _____.
    a. the definition of proper behavior in particular circumstances so that everyone is clear about their rights and duties
    b. protecting the wealthy from the poor
    c. redefining what is proper behavior when situations change
    d. allocating authority to use coercion to enforce sanctions
    e. "the definition of proper behavior in particular circumstances so that everyone is clear about their rights and duties", "redefining what is proper behavior when situations change" and "allocating authority to use coercion to enforce sanctions"

15. A method of resolving disputes in which the disputing parties voluntarily arrive at a mutually satisfactory agreement is called _____.
    a. negotiation
    b. mediation
    c. adjudication
    d. use of sanctions
    e. law

16. Which of the following are likely to be associated with warfare?

    a. centralized political systems

    b. the rise of cities

    c. a technology that supports population growth

    d. possession of complex, valuable property

    e. "centralized political systems", "the rise of cities", "a technology that supports population growth" and "possession of complex, valuable property"

17. An exploitative world view is more likely to exist in which of the following technologies?

    a. food foraging

    b. horticulture

    c. pastoralism

    d. intensive agriculture

    e. horticulture, pastoralism and intensive agriculture

18. Power based on force does not usually last very long; to be effective, it must be considered _____.

    a. legitimate

    b. mediated

    c. negotiated

    d. subject to sanctions

    e. inevitable

19. _____, which seem to be associated with the weak and with dependents, provides one of several checks on the abuse of authority in Bedouin society.

    a. Ostracism

    b. Informal sanctions

    c. Legal sanctions

    d. Paralegal sanctions

    e. Supernatural sanctions

20. Another agent of control in societies, whether or not they possess centralized political systems, may be _____.

    a. witchcraft

    b. sorcerers

    c. ostracism

    d. fines set by judges

    e. warriors

21. An important pioneer in the anthropological study of law was _____.

    a. A.L. Kroeber

    b. George Peter Murdock

    c. John Wesley Powell

    d. E. Adamson Hoebel

    e. Peggy Reeves Sanday

22. The field of _____ is one of growing anthropological involvement and employment.

    a. ethnoscience

    b. ethnology

    c. dispute control

    d. dispute management

    e. assertiveness training

23. In 1980 _____, as a practitioner of dispute management, helped the U.S. and the Soviet Union replace their obsolete "hot line" with fully equipped nuclear crisis centers in each capital.

    a. Sue Ellen Jacobs

    b. William L. Ury

    c. Laura Nader

    d. L. Abu-Lughod

    e. Harald Prins

24. When one refers to the way power is distributed and embedded in society, one is referring to a society's _____.

    a. social organization

    b. military structure

    c. political ideology

    d. class structure

    e. political organization

25. The ability to control others' behavior, whether organizing a seal hunt or raising a military force, has to do with the way power is distributed and embedded in a society, or its _____.

    a. political organization

    b. social class structure

    c. political ideology

    d. police force

    e. social system

26. To support the view that humans are innately warlike observers cite the behavior of people such as the _____, who are portrayed as living in a constant state of war.

    a. Apache

    b. Comanche

    c. Ju/'hoansi

    d. Mende

    e. Yanomami

27. It is clear that war is not a universal phenomenon, for in various parts of the world there are societies that do not practice warfare as we know it. Which of the following groups of people is **not** an example of a group that does not practice warfare?

    a. the Bushman of southern Africa

    b. the Arapesh of New Guinea

    c. the Hopi of the American southwest

    d. the Yanomami of South America

    e. all are warlike; the Bushman of southern Africa, the Arapesh of New Guinea, the Hopi of the American southwest and the Yanomami of South America

28. Scholars have identified four basic kinds of political systems and categorized them into uncentralized and centralized. Which of the following would be considered uncentralized systems?

    a. chiefdoms

    b. tribes

    c. states

    d. bands

    e. tribes and bands

29. The _____ do not think of government as something fixed and all-powerful, and to them leadership was not vested in a central authority.

    a. Navajo

    b. Melanesians

    c. Mayan

    d. Yanomami

    e. Gururumba

30. In his classic study of segmentary lineage organizations, Marshall Sahlins described how this system works among the _____.

    a. Kapauku

    b. Nuer

    c. Tiriki

    d. Ju/'hoansi

    e. Onondaga

31. _____ systems provide a tribal society with a means of political integration beyond the kin group.

    a. Age-grade

    b. Common-interest association

    c. Segmentary lineage

    d. Kindred

    e. Clan

32. An important pioneer in the anthropological study of law was _____.

    a. E.E. Evans-Pritchard

    b. Marshal Sahlins

    c. Leo Pospisil

    d. E. Adamson Hoebel

    e. A.R. Radcliffe-Brown

33. Although leaders of chiefdoms are almost always men, in some cultures a politically astute wife, sister, or single daughter of a deceased male chief could inherit that position. One historical example is Queen _____who succeeded her half brother as leader of the Polynesian chiefdom of Tahiti in 1827.

    a. Liliokalnai

    b. Latifah

    c. Wilhelmina

    d. Pomare IV

    e. Isabella

34. _____ is a new state that was formed after an armed struggle with Yugoslavia.

    a. Suriname

    b. Bosnia

    c. Croatia

    d. East Timor

    e. Kurdistan

35. Some nations have forged their own states without open violence, such was the case with _____, a former Dutch colony on the northeast coast of South America.

    a. Suriname

    b. Belice

    c. Curacao

    d. Guyana

    e. Trinidad

36. In the past 5,000 years or so, there have been more than _____ wars, resulting in many hundreds of millions of casualties.
    a. 1,000
    b. 5,000
    c. 14,000
    d. 20,000
    e. 12,000

37. Many armies around the world recruit children. Today, there are more than _____ child soldiers, many as young as 12-15 years-old.
    a. 25,000
    b. 100,000
    c. 300,000
    d. 1,000,000
    e. 50,000

38. Playing a leading role in the development of the anthropology of law, _____ has taken on specialists in the fields of law, children's issues, nuclear energy, and science, critically questioning the basic assumptions under which these experts operate.
    a. Ralph Nader
    b. Margaret Mead
    c. Martha Knack
    d. Laura Nader
    e. Ruth Benedict

True/False Practice Questions

1. In the French monarchy under Louis XIV, the king was the state in an important sense.
   True or False

2. Until recently many non-Western peoples had no fixed form of government in the sense that Westerners understand the term.
   True or False

3. The Ju/'hoansi have a tribal-type political organization.
   True or False

4. The Big Man of the Kapauku is called tonowi.
   True or False

5. A classic example of a segmentary lineage system is found among the Nuer.
   True or False

6. In Bedouin society, because those in authority are expected to treat their dependents with some respect, they must draw as little attention as possible to the inequality of their relationship.
   True or False

7. The use of fictive kin terms serves to mask relations of inequality in Bedouin society.
   True or False

8. Among the Bedouins, the tyranny of those in power is accepted as natural and tolerated.
   True or False

9. A Bedouin woman can resist a tyrannical husband by leaving for her natal home "angry." This is the approved response to abuse in Bedouin society.
   True or False

10. Bedouin women have less recourse against tyrannical fathers or guardians, but various informal means to resist the imposition of unwanted decisions do exist. Although, suicide is not one of them.
    True or False

11. Figures of authority in Bedouin society are vulnerable to their dependents because their positions rest on the respect these people are willing to give them.
    True or False

12. What anthropologists involved with dispute management are trying to do is to help create a culture of negotiation in a world where adversarial, win-lose attitudes are out of step with the increasingly interdependent relations between people.
    True or False

13. The term political organization refers to the way power is distributed and embedded in society.
    True or False

14. It is clear that war is a universal phenomena.
    True or False

15. Among food foragers, with their uncentralized political systems, warfare is all but unknown.
    True or False

16. Among the Igbo of Midwestern Nigeria, women were not allowed positions in the administrative hierarchy.
    True or False

17. Western societies do not clearly distinguish offenses against the state, called crimes, from offenses against individuals, called torts.
    True or False

18. Every society develops customs designed to encourage conformity to social norms.
    True or False

19. To a greater or lesser extent, political organizations all over the world seek to legitimize their power through recourse to supernatural ideas.
    True or False

20. Many contemporary wars are not between states but often occur within countries where the government is either corrupt, ineffective, or without popular support.
    True or False

Practice Matching

1. _____ Nuer
2. _____ Swazi
3. _____ Igbo
4. _____ Wape
5. _____ Abenaki

a. Nigerian society in which men and women occupy separate political spheres.
b. Northeastern Native American foragers in the historic past that lived in harmony with their environment.
c. A southeast African nation.
d. A New Guinea people in the historical past with effective informal and internalized controls.
e. East African herders with a segmentary lineage system.

Short Answer

1. Why is it incorrect to blame political unrest in many parts of the world on "tribalism?"

2. Identify the countries where women have recently been elected and served as presidents or prime ministers.

3. The "Bearver Wars" took place during the 16th century in the American northeast. Explain why they occurred.

4. Explain how the Iroquois Confederacy came into being.

Practice Essays

1. Why has the state-type system expanded to encompass most of the globe today? Explore how band, tribe, and chiefdom organizations might persist within a world order based primarily on states.

2. Identify and discuss the limits on the power of authority figures in Bedouin society. That is, what options are open to dependents in Bedouin society that would allow them to check an oppressive authority figure?

3. Who is William L. Ury? What is his area of expertise? What is he trying to accomplish?

4. Describe how the segmentary lineage system works among the Nuer.

5. Why do wars occur? Is the need to wage war an instinctive feature of the human personality? Explain.

6. One of the state's responsibilities is the organization and execution of war. Explain why states revert to war.

7. Describe the Aztec wars and the Christian Crusades and discuss the motivations and justifications for the aggressive behavior of those two groups.

Solutions

Fill-in-the-Blank

1. political organization
2. government
3. uncentralized, centralized
4. band
5. 10,000
6. Ju/'hoansi
7. consensus
8. tribe
9. segmentary
10. leopard-skin chief
11. Big Man
12. chiefdom
13. redistributive
14. state
15. intensive
16. Iroquois
17. ghosts
18. internal
19. superntural
20. song duels
21. rules of custom
22. criminal, civil
23. negotiation, mediation
24. state

Multiple-Choice Practice Questions

1. E
2. D
3. E
4. D
5. D
6. C
7. B
8. D
9. E
10. A
11. C
12. D
13. D
14. E
15. A
16. E
17. E
18. A
19. E
20. A
21. D
22. D
23. B
24. E
25. A
26. E
27. D
28. E
29. A
30. B
31. A
32. D
33. D
34. B
35. A
36. C
37. C
38. D

True/False Practice Questions

1. T
2. T
3. F
4. T
5. T
6. T
7. T
8. F
9. T
10. T
11. T
12. T
13. T
14. F
15. T
16. F
17. F
18. T
19. T
20. T

Practice Matching

1. E
2. C
3. A
4. D
5. B

197

Chapter 13

Spirituality, Religion, and the Supernatural

Synopsis

In Chapter 13 the text discusses the universality of religion, considering the functions served by religious belief and ritual in the social order. Various kinds of supernatural beings are compared and the relationships among magic, science, and religion are examined. The role of religion in culture change is also discussed.

What You Should Learn from This Chapter

I.   Understand why religion exists

II.   Understand the various forms of religious belief:

    A.   animatism

    B.   animism

    C.   shamanism

    D.   belief in ancestral spirits

    E.   belief in gods and goddesses

III.   Understand the relationship between religion, magic, and witchcraft and the functions of each.

IV.   Understand the role of religion in cultural change.

Key Terms and Names

animatism
animism
contagious magic
divination
Edward B. Tylor
imitative magic
incorporation
pantheon
polytheism
priest or priestess

religion
revitalization movements
rites of intensification
rites of passage
separation
shaman
spirituality
transition
witchcraft
worldview

Exercise

Briefly identify and locate the following cultures discussed in the chapter.

1. Tewa

2. Sioux

3. Ibibio

4. Mende

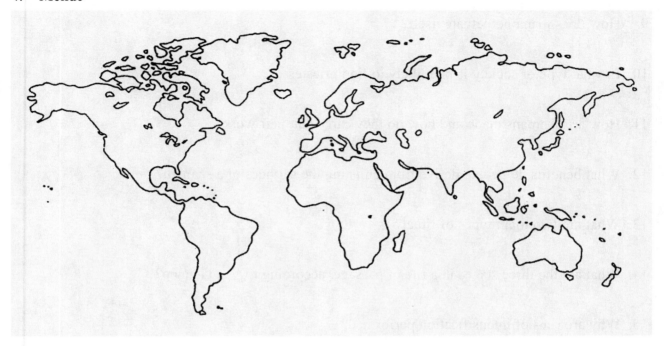

Exercise

Review Questions

1. What is the relationship between science and religion?

2. Why might there be less religion, as defined in your textbook, in more complex societies?

3. What are three categories of supernatural beings?

4. What is the role of gods and goddesses in many societies?

5. How does healing occur among the Ju/'hoansi?

6. What purpose do ancestral spirits serve?

7. In what type of society is one likely to find animism?

8. Distinguish between animism and animatism.

9. How does mana perpetuate itself?

10. In what type of society is one likely to find priestesses?

11. How are shamans made and how do they carry out their work?

12. What benefits do people derive from enlisting the services of a shaman?

13. What are two main types of ritual?

14. What are the three stages in a rite of passage, according to Van Gennep?

15. Why are rites of intensification performed?

16. Distinguish between the two fundamental principles of magic.

17. In what ways does the Tewa origin myth reflect Tewa social structure?

18. How are witch hunts used for societal control?

19. What is the role of witchcraft among the Navajo?

20. What are the psychological functions of religion?

21. What are the social functions of religion?

22. How and why do revitalization movements emerge?

Fill-in-the-Blank

1. Alfonso Ortiz was an anthropologist of _____ ancestry who studied the religious beliefs of the Tewa.

2. In Tewa society the _____ mediate between the human and spiritual worlds and between the two moieties.

3. In the nineteenth century European thinkers believed that _____ would eventually eclipse religion.

4. The set of gods and goddesses in a society are called its _____ .

5. In most societies with subsistence bases in _____ or _____ , deities are conceptualized as masculine.

6. A belief that nature is animated by spirits is called _____ .

7. A concept of impersonal power, such as mana, is called _____ .

8. _____ are specialists who have acquired spiritual power, which they can use on behalf of human clients.

9. _____ was a pioneer in the study of rites of passage.

10. When Mende girls are initiated into adult society, they undergo _____ .

11. A ceremony to bring rain to a drought-stricken community is a _____ .

12. The three stages of a life crisis ritual are _____ , _____ , and _____ .

13. _____ wrote The Golden Bough.

14. _____ magic is based on the assumption that things that are similar to each other have an effect on each other.

15. Assuming that a person's fingernail clippings, hair, blood, and so on retain a spiritual connection to that person is the basis for _____ magic.

16. Among the Navajo, _____ is a way of expression and channeling hostile feelings.

17. A _____ is a social movement whose intent is to totally transform a society.

Multiple-Choice Practice Questions

1. Islamic fundamentalism in Iran and Christian fundamentalism in the United States demonstrate that _____.
   a. science has succeeded in destroying religion in the twentieth century
   b. religious activity is prominent in the lives of social elites.
   c. science meets basic needs
   d. religion is a powerful and dynamic force in society today
   e. science is wrong

2. _____ may be defined as the beliefs and patterns of behavior by which people try to control those aspects of the universe that are otherwise beyond their control.
   a. Political organization
   b. Government
   c. Kinship
   d. Common-interest associations
   e. Religion

3. Which of the following is **least** likely to be extensively involved in religious beliefs and activities?

    a. single women with ten children living below the poverty line, who dropped out of school at age fourteen

    b. members of food-foraging societies with limited scientific knowledge

    c. peasants in a feudal society

    d. members of lower classes in an urban-industrial society

    e. wealthy members of urban-industrial societies with advanced scientific knowledge

4. A people's collection of gods and goddesses is called a _____.

    a. mana

    b. shaman

    c. pantheon

    d. priest

    e. fetish

5. Belief in a supreme being who controls the universe is usually associated with _____.

    a. bands

    b. tribes

    c. chiefdoms

    d. states

    e. multinational corporations

6. If religious belief reflects the structure of society, in which types of society would you expect to find widespread belief in ancestral spirits?

    a. those in which descent groups play a major role in social organization

    b. those with a disproportionately large number of old people

    c. those with a disproportionately large number of young people

    d. those in which neolocal marital residence are the rule

    e. those with egocentric systems such as the kindred

7. The belief that nature is animated with spirits is called _____.

    a. animation

    b. anima

    c. animatism

    d. animism

    e. ennui

8. A _____ is a full-time religious specialist who occupies an office that has a certain rank and function.

    a. shaman

    b. priest

    c. witch

    d. magician

    e. diviner

9. In acting as a healer, the shaman _____.

    a. accurately diagnoses medical problems

    b. may improve the patient's state of mind, which aids in recovery

    c. may be coping with his or her own problems by becoming intensely involved with the problems of others

    d. provides reassurance to the community through an elaborate drama that may involve trickery

    e. "may improve the patient's state of mind, which aids in recovery", "may be coping with his or her own problems by becoming intensely involved with the problems of others" and "provides reassurance to the community through an elaborate drama that may involve trickery"

10. Ceremonies such as bar mitzvah, elaborate wedding ceremonies, baby showers, and graduation parties that help individuals make major changes in their lives are referred to as rites of _____.

    a. transition

    b. intensification

    c. separation

    d. passage

    e. incorporation

11. A funeral ceremony may be regarded as _____.

    a. a rite of passage

    b. an opportunity to restore the equilibrium of the group

    c. an opportunity for individuals to express their feelings in a structured way that ensures continuation of society

    d. a rite of intensification

    e. "a rite of passage", "an opportunity to restore the equilibrium of the group", "an opportunity for individuals to express their feelings in a structured way that ensures continuation of society" and "a rite of intensification"

12. In *The Golden Bough*, _____ distinguished between religion and magic.

    a. Bronislaw Malinowski

    b. Franz Boas

    c. Sir James Frazer

    d. Sir Edward Tylor

    e. Clifford Geertz

13. Many magical incantations require the use of fingernail clippings of the intended victim. This is an example of _____.

    a. imitative magic

    b. contagious magic

    c. witch magic

    d. nightmare magic

    e. scientific thinking

14. Magic involves the manipulation of powers for good or evil, whereas witchcraft involves the possession of an innate power used for _____.

    a. religious purposes

    b. scientific reasons

    c. malevolent or benevolent purposes

    d. traditional societies

    e. societies that lack religion

15. Religion, magic, and witchcraft are all **similar** in which of the following ways?

    a. They all disappear once modern education and scientific training expand

    b. They all share the common goal of improving social relationships within a community

    c. They are all associated with morose nonconformists who try to destroy society

    d. They provide explanations of events and are mechanisms of social control

    e. They are all morally neutral

16. A belief in _____ enables people to explain why things go wrong by blaming certain individuals who are said to have the internal psychic ability to cause harm to others.

    a. witchcraft

    b. magic

    c. divination

    d. contagion

    e. evil

17. Which of the following illustrate the psychological functions of religion?

    a. Among the Holy Ghost People of the United States, handling snakes and drinking strychnine is a common feature of their worship; one explanation of this behavior is that by confronting the possibility of death, they achieve a sense of awe and transcendence

    b. An Islamic judge who orders the hand of a thief cut off can sleep soundly at night because he thinks of himself as merely the agent of divinely inspired justice

    c. The Tewa Indian origin myth provides every Tewa with a sense of this place in an orderly universe

    d. A person raised in the Catholic religion feels tremendous guilt when she/he commits a wrong

    e. "Among the Holy Ghost People of the United States, handling snakes and drinking strychnine is a common feature of their worship; one explanation of this behavior is that by confronting the possibility of death, they achieve a sense of awe and transcendence" "An Islamic judge who orders the hand of a thief cut off can sleep soundly at night because he thinks of himself as merely the agent of divinely inspired justice" and "The Tewa Indian origin myth provides every Tewa with a sense of this place in an orderly universe"

18. A _____ is a deliberate effort by members of a society to construct a more satisfying culture.

    a. divination

    b. rite of intensification

    c. fetish

    d. segmentary lineage system

    e. revitalization movement

19. Which of the following statements about revitalization movements is **incorrect**?

    a. The purpose of revitalization movements is to reform society

    b. Revitalization movements always fail because they require too much change to be tolerated

    c. All known major religions, including Judaism, Christianity, and Islam, began as revitalization movements

    d. Revitalization movements may be completely unrealistic

    e. Revitalization movements may be adaptive and give rise to long-lasting religions

20. N/um generally remains dormant in a healer until an effort is made to activate it. Among the ways to activate n/um are _____.

    a. trance dance

    b. hallucinogenic drugs

    c. medicinal curing ceremony

    d. solo singing

    e. trance dance, medicinal curing ceremony and solo singing

21. In southern Africa's Swaziland all types of illnesses are generally thought to be caused by
_____ or _____.
    a. viruses/bacteria
    b. negative karma/negative attitude
    c. sorcery/loss of ancestral protection
    d. poor hygiene/poverty
    e. none of these

22. Which of the following have the Swazi **not** traditionally relied upon for treatment of disease?
    a. herbalists
    b. diviner mediums
    c. Christian faith healers
    d. general practitioners
    e. they rely on all of these; herbalists, diviner mediums, Christian faith healers and general practitioners

23. In a country where there is one traditional healer for every 110 people, but only one physician for every 10,000, the potential benefit of cooperation between physicians and healers seems self-evident. However, it was unrecognized until proposed by anthropologist _____.
    a. Edward C. Green
    b. Harald Prins
    c. Sir Edward B. Tylor
    d. William L. Ury
    e. R.R. Marett

24. Religion is viewed most simply as organized belief in the _____, and all fulfill numerous social and psychological needs.
    a. Christianity
    b. social system
    c. supernatural
    d. prevailing culture
    e. magic

25. _____ is considered a "New Age" religion.
    a. Wicca
    b. Reform Judaism
    c. New Catholicism
    d. Seventh Day Adventist
    e. Whateverism

26. In addition to so-called "New Age" enthusiasts, faith healers and many other evangelists among fundamentalist Christians share most of the characteristics of _____.

    a. Buddhism

    b. Shintoism

    c. Taoism

    d. shamanism

    e. socialism

27. The meanings ascribed to sensations experienced in altered states and made of their content are _____ determined; hence local traditions always vary in their detail.

    a. politically

    b. economically

    c. biologically

    d. culturally

    e. hallucinagenically

28. In 1996, a Gallup poll found that _____ percent of the respondents believed that it might be possible that the dead might be able to contact the living.

    a. 22

    b. 5

    c. 50

    d. 42

    e. 12

29. Anthropologist _____ defined religion as "a set of rituals, rationalized by myth, which mobilizes supernatural powers for the purpose of achieving or preventing transformations of state in man and nature."

    a. E.E. Evans-Pritchard

    b. E. Adamson Hoebel

    c. Hilda Kuper

    d. A.R. Radcliffe-Brown

    e. Anthony F.C. Wallace

30. The _____ Indians maintained that each person had a personal spirit that could detach itself and travel about apart from the body, while the latter remained inert.

    a. Cayuga

    b. Hopi

    c. Cheyenne

    d. Penobscot

    e. Mayan

31. In the United States millions of people have learned something about shamans through reading _____ accounts of his experiences with Don Juan, the Yaqui Indian shaman.

    a. R.R. Marett's

    b. Carlos Castaneda's

    c. Edward B. Tylor's

    d. Laura Nader's

    e. Colin Turnbull's

32. The rites of passage that help individuals through the crucial crisis of their lives can be divided into three stages. Which of the following would be those stages?

    a. separation

    b. transition

    c. incorporation

    d. acquisition

    e. separation, transition and incorporation

33. Widely known among American Indians are the _____, who possess a detailed concept of witchcraft.

    a. Algonkian

    b. Cree

    c. Gros Ventre

    d. Navajo

    e. Shoshone

34. In the United States, _____ is an example of a revitalization movement that is enormously successful in gaining acceptance in the wider society.

    a. the Unification Church

    b. Mormonism

    c. the Branch Davidian

    d. the Heaven's Gate cult

    e. Jonestown

35. _____ forms part of a cultural system's superstructure, which comprises a society's worldview.

    a. Political philosophy

    b. Economic organization

    c. Social structure

    d. Religion

    e. The arts

36. Followers of _____in the U.S. today number 800,000.
    a. Islam
    b. Buddhism
    c. Hinduism
    d. Judaism
    e. Wicca

37. Which of the following is considered a "New Age" religion and has 310,000 adherents today?
    a. Lutheran
    b. Buddhism
    c. Shintoism
    d. Wicca
    e. Holy Rollers

True/False Practice Questions

1. The belief that nature is animated by spirits is called animism.
   True or False

2. Rituals reinforce social solidarity and thus enable individuals and groups to get through crisis.
   True or False

3. Rites of intensification help individuals get through a crisis.
   True or False

4. Religion provides an orderly model of the universe and reduces fear and anxiety.
   True or False

5. Interceding with the spirits and drawing out their invisible arrows is the task of (Ju/'hoansi) healers.
   True or False

6. Among the Ju/'hoansi only men can possess the powerful healing force called *n/um*.
   True or False

7. *N/um* is the Ju/'hoansi equivalent of *mana*.
   True or False

8. The trances that healers go into are considered harmless; they simply lose consciousness.
   True or False

9. The power of healers' n/um is all that is thought to protect the healer in a trance from actual death.
   True or False

10. Today biomedical germ theory is universally accepted in societies around the world.
    True or False

11. Religion is viewed most simply as organized belief in the supernatural that does not fulfill any social and psychological needs.
    True or False

12. Science, with its creation of new technologies, has helped diminish religious practice in the United States.
    True or False

13. Faith healers and many other evangelists among fundamentalist Christians have nothing in common with shamanism.
    True or False

14. The meanings ascribed to sensations experienced in altered states and made of their content are culturally determined.
    True or False

15. In fact, the custom of clitoridectomy is practiced by some in New York State.
    True or False

16. Far from causing the death of religion, the growth of scientific knowledge, by producing new anxieties and raising new questions about human existence, may have contributed to the continuing practice of religion in modern life.
    True or False

17. Religion is a part of all known cultures.
    True or False

18. The patriarchal nature of Western society is expressed in its theology.
    True or False

19. Shamanism is absent in modern industrial societies like the United States.
    True or False

20. In an attempt to deal with problems that defy ordinary explanation or solutions through material means, people appeal to, or seek influence and even manipulate spiritual or supernatural beings and powers.
    True or False

21. As pointed out in the textbook, people often turn to religion in the hope of reaching a specific goal, such as the healing of physical, emotional, or social ills.
    True or False

Practice Matching

Match the culture with its characteristic.

1. _____ Navajo
2. _____ Tewa
3. _____ Ibibio
4. _____ Sioux
5. _____ Mende

a. West African people who practice female initiation rite involving clitoridectomy.
b. Southwestern Native Americans with a witchcraft tradition.
c. Native Americans of the plains who started the Ghost Dance as a religious revitalization.
d. Native Americans of New Mexico whose origin myth reflects and validates their social structure.
e. Sub-Saharan African people with a witchcraft tradition.

Short Answer

1. Discuss the essence of the Tewa worldview.

2. Is there a difference between religion and spirituality? If so, what is it?

3. What is the anthropological definition of the term "shaman."

Practice Essays

1. Bronislaw Malinowski, in his classic essay *Magic, Science, and Religion*, claimed that each of these was a viable mode of cognition and that most societies exhibit all of them in variable proportions. In what ways does magical thinking persist in contemporary North America? Is it likely to persist into the future?

2. Identify and describe the various ways the Jo/'hoansi activate the powerful healing force called n/um.

3. How is modern medicine reconciled with traditional beliefs in Swaziland?

4. What is shamanism and how can the widespread occurrence of shamanism be explained?

5. Religious rituals are religion in action. Describe what in fact is accomplished by religious rituals.

6. What is a revitalization movement? Explain how and why do they come into existence?

Solutions

Fill-in-the-Blank

1. Tewa
2. priests
3. science
4. pantheon
5. pastoralism, intensive agriculture
6. animism
7. animatism
8. Shaman
9. Arnold Van Gennep
10. clitoridectomy
11. rite of intensification
12. separation, transition, incorporation
13. Sir James George Frazer
14. Imitative
15. contagious
16. witchcraft
17. revitalization movement

Multiple-Choice Practice Questions

1. D
2. E
3. E
4. C
5. D
6. A
7. D
8. B
9. E
10. D
11. E
12. C
13. B
14. C
15. D
16. A
17. E
18. E
19. B
20. E
21. C
22. D
23. A
24. C
25. A
26. D
27. D
28. A
29. E
30. D
31. B
32. E
33. D
34. B
35. D
36. C
37. D

True/False Practice Questions

1. T
2. T
3. F
4. T
5. T
6. F
7. T
8. F
9. T
10. F
11. F
12. F
13. F
14. T
15. T
16. T
17. T
18. T
19. F
20. T
21. T

Practice Matching

1. B
2. D
3. E
4. C
5. A

Chapter 14

The Arts

Synopsis

Chapter 14 examines the ethnocentric assumptions implicit in most Western definitions of the arts and artists. It distinguishes different types of creative activity such as the verbal arts, music, and sculpture and attempts to come up with a cross-culturally valid definition of art.

What You Should Learn from This Chapter

I.   Understand why anthropologists are interested in the arts.

II.   Understand the forms of verbal arts and how they function in society:

    A.   myth

    B.   legend

    C.   tale

III. Understand the function of music.

IV.   Understand the range of visual and plastic arts in human societies.

Key Terms

art   iconic images
construal   legend
entopic phenomena   motif
epic   myth
ethnomusicology   tale
folklore   tonality
folkloristics

Exercise

Review Questions

1.   Distinguish between secular and religious art.

2.   What are the basic kinds of verbal arts studied by anthropologists?

3.   Give an example of how myth expresses the world view of a people.

4.   Distinguish between legend and myth.

5. Why is matriarchy a common theme in many societies' myths?

6. What role does poetry play in the lives of the Bedouins?

7. What type of society is likely to have epics? Why?

8. What aspects of legends are of interest to anthropologists?

9. Why are anthropologists interested in tales?

10. What are the functions of music?

11. Distinguish between art and craft.

12. What is the importance of entopic phenomena?

13. What is the "second stage" of trance?

14. Are there any universal characteristics of art?

15. Why do marketing experts routinely employ music and pictorial images in their advertising?

Fill-in-the-Blank

1. The term "verbal arts" is preferred to the term _____ , a term developed in the nineteenth century to refer to traditional oral stories of European peasants.

2. The word "myth," in _____ usage, refers to something that is widely believed to be true but isn't.

3. Tabaldak and Odziozo are characters in the origin myth of the _____ .

4. Legends are _____ narratives that recount the deeds of heroes, the movements of people, and the establishment of customs.

5. Studies of tales in the southeast United States now indicate that they originated in _____ rather than Europe.

6. "Little songs" that occur every day were studied among the _____ .

7. The study of music in its cultural setting is called _____ .

8. The term _____ is used to refer to scale systems and their modifications in music.

9. An alternative to the Western octave system is the _____ , which is defined by five equidistant tones.

10. Two people playing different patterns of beats at the same time is called _____ .

11. The cultures of _____ have a particularly rich tradition of sculpture.

12. Among the Pomo Indians of California, _____ is an important expression of aesthetic interest.

13. The human nervous system produces images out of which patterns are construed. These are called _____ .

Multiple-Choice Practice Questions

1. Whether useful or non-useful, all art is an expression of _____.

    a. the innate need to be impractical

    b. a fundamental human capacity for religious expression

    c. state-level societies that can afford specialists

    d. political domination of minorities by elites

    e. the symbolic representation of form and the expression of feeling that constitutes creativity

2. The observation that all cultures include activities that provide aesthetic pleasure suggests that _____.

    a. humans may have an innate or acquired need to produce art

    b. the human mind requires the stimulation of imaginative play to prevent boredom

    c. all societies, from food-foraging bands to industrial states, include art in their culture

    d. art is a necessary activity in which all normal, active members of society participate

    e. "humans may have an innate or acquired need to produce art", "the human mind requires the stimulation of imaginative play to prevent boredom", "all societies, from food-foraging bands to industrial states, include art in their culture" and "art is a necessary activity in which all normal, active members of society participate"

3. Anthropologists prefer to use the term *verbal arts* rather than the term *folklore* because the term _____.

    a. *folklore* is used only by linguists; the term *verbal arts* is used only by anthropologists

    b. *verbal arts* sounds more sophisticated

    c. *verbal arts* is more scientific

    d. *folklore* implies lack of sophistication and is a condescending term to use

    e. *folklore* refers only to fairy tales

4. The type of verbal arts that has received the most study and attention is _____.
    a. poetry
    b. incantations
    c. narratives
    d. proverbs
    e. riddles

5. In the myth of Tabaldak and Odziozo, Tabaldak first created the Abenakis from stone and then from living wood. What does this tell us about the functions of myth?
    a. Myths function to tell actual history; the Abenakis believe that they were originally made of wood
    b. Myths bring humor into the lives of the Abenakis because the myths are so ridiculous
    c. Myths function primarily to provide entertainment; the Abnakis know they were not made from wood, but like to tell this story to visiting anthropologists who are so gullible
    d. Myths function to express a culture's world view; the Abenakis see themselves as belonging to the world of living things rather than to the nonliving world of stone
    e. Myths provide skills of woodworking and stone masonry to the Abenakis

6. Because legends contain details of a people's past, they are a form of history; because they often give a picture of a people's view of the world and humanity's place in it, they are like _____.
    a. poetry
    b. religion
    c. magic
    d. kinship systems
    e. myths

7. When an anthropologist uses the term _____, he or she is referring to a category of verbal narratives that are secular, non-historical, and seen primarily as a source of entertainment.
    a. "folklore"
    b. "myth"
    c. "tale"
    d. "legend"
    e. "drama"

8. Your text describes a type of narrative found in many cultures in which a peasant father and his son, while traveling with their beast of burden, meet a number of people who criticize them. What is the motif?
    a. The "motif" refers to the psychological motives of the characters in a story, in this case the desire of the son to do better than his father.
    b. "Motif" means the historical background to the story, in this case the history of exploitation of the peasantry.
    c. The "motif" refers to the story situation, in this case a father and son trying to please everyone.
    d. "Motif" means the physical environment in which the story occurs, in this case the yam gardens of Ghana.
    e. The "motif" refers to the economic background, in this case feudalism.

9. The "little songs" of the Bedouin are considered un-Islamic; they are the discourse of children, used to express rebellious ideas and feelings. Thus they are _____.
    a. anti-structural
    b. forbidden
    c. sung among Europeans only
    d. sung only when the Bedouins are away from their homeland
    e. sung only at marriages

10. The field of ethnomusicology _____.
    a. is concerned with human music rather than natural music
    b. is the study of music in its cultural setting
    c. began in the nineteenth century with the collection of folk songs
    d. concerns the organization of melody, rhythm, and form in a culture's music
    e. "is concerned with human music rather than natural music", "is the study of music in its cultural setting", "began in the nineteenth century with the collection of folk songs" and "concerns the organization of melody, rhythm, and form in a culture's music"

11. Scale systems and their modifications in music are called _____.
    a. tonality
    b. ethnomusicology
    c. sculpture
    d. verbal arts
    e. pentatonic

12. During the Washington Peace March in the sixties, thousands of people sang the song "We Shall Overcome." This song expressed a feeling of common purpose to counteract repression and to reform society. It created a sense of unity among diverse members of the crowd. This example illustrates the _____ of music.

    a. social functions

    b. geographical distribution

    c. tonality

    d. mythological features

    e. polyrhythms

13. Objects that are trivial, low in symbolic content, or impermanent are usually considered products of _____.

    a. an ethnomusicologist

    b. a tale

    c. craft

    d. art

    e. sculpture

14. Amongst the Kalahari groups of the 1950s and 1960s, about half the men and a third of the women were _____.

    a. rock artists

    b. shaman

    c. hunters

    d. gatherers

    e. chiefs

15. For this group of Native Americans basketmaking has been important for their sense of who they are since before European contact.

    a. Cheyenne

    b. Hurok

    c. Pomo

    d. Chumash

    e. Comanche

16. After comprehensive archaeological, ethnographic, and other studies were completed, anthropologist _____ succeeded in having the Pomo basketry materials recognized National Register of Historic Places as "historic property."

    a. Richard N. Lerner

    b. Edward C. Green

    c. L. Abu-Lughod

    d. William L. Ury

    e. G. Koch

17. As the British anthropologist Raymond Firth observed: "_____ is an art of making sense out of experience, and like any other art, say, poetry, it must be taken symbolically, not literally."

    a. Entertainment

    b. Music

    c. Dance

    d. Religion

    e. Painting

18. In the United States numerous examples exist of marginalized social and ethnic groups attempting to gain a larger audience and more compassion for their plight through song. Perhaps no better example exists than _____.

    a. Mexican Americans

    b. Chinese Americans

    c. Native Americans

    d. Puerto Ricans

    e. African Americans

    A surprisingly large number of _____ in European and African tales are traceable to ancient sources in India.

    stories

    myths

    motifs

    devices

    ies

    of the following music forms emerged out of the African American experience in the
    tates?

    n 19
    d by t

    formers like Elvis Presley and Pat Boone have in common?

    nfluenced by African American music

    own music

    vn lyrics

    own versions of African American music to Black audiences

    wn versions of African American music to White audiences

22. Perhaps the oldest form of artistic expression is _____.

    a. oil painting

    b. sculpting

    c. pottery

    d. body decoration

    e. cave drawings

23. A true _____ is basically religious, in that it provides a rationale for religious beliefs and practices.

    a. folktale

    b. legend

    c. myth

    d. epic tale

    e. riddle

24. Much of what passes for history, consists of the _____ we develop to make ourselves feel better about who we are.

    a. poems

    b. parables

    c. legends

    d. ballads

    e. fictions

25. A surprisingly large number of motifs in European and African tales are traceable to ancient sources in _____.

    a. China

    b. Japan

    c. Latin America

    d. India

    e. Mesopotamia

26. Applying the interpretive approach to southern African rock art requires knowledge of which two subjects?

    a. Mbuti ethnography

    b. Busman ethnography

    c. nature of the rain forest

    d. nature of the trance

    e. Busman ethnography and nature of the trance

27. _____ serves as a powerful way for a social or ethnic group to assert its distinctive identity.
    a. Tales
    b. Music
    c. Chants
    d. Poems
    e. Plays

28. Art can affirm group solidarity and identity beyond kinship lines as evidenced by the United State's _____.
    a. turkey
    b. crescent moon.
    c. cedar tree.
    d. maple leaf.
    e. bald eagle.

29. The cedar tree is _____'s symbol of group solidarity and identity.
    a. Canada
    b. Italy
    c. Jordan
    d. Lebanon
    e. Syria

30. Tattoos in the U.S. have traveled a long way from the tattoo of old: brought to North America by way of _____'s 18th century of the Pacific.
    a. Christopher Columbus
    b. Sir Francis Drake
    c. Captain James Cook
    d. Ferdinand Magellan
    e. Juan Cabrillo

True/False Practice Questions

1. The term "tale" refers to a type of narrative that is secular, non-historical, and seen primarily as a source of entertainment.
   True or False

2. Legends are semi-historical narratives which recount the deeds of heroes, the movement of peoples and the establishment of local customs.
   True or False

3. The word "myth," in popular usage, refers to something that is widely believed to be true but probably isn't.
   True or False

4. Legends provide clues as to what is considered appropriate behavior in a culture.
   True or False

5. Bushman rock images are banal, meaningless artifacts akin to urban graffiti in the U.S.
    True or False

6. Bushman art has a single, one-to-one 'meaning' that it unequivocally transmits from the maker to the viewer.
    True or False

7. Bushman rock art were simply records of religious experiences.
    True or False

8. Bushman rock art were not just pictures, but rather powerful things in themselves that could facilitate the mediation of the cosmological realms.
    True or False

9. Bushman rock art were just pictures that had no power to effect changes in the shamans' states of consciousness.
    True or False

10. The making of art was, for the Bushman, an idle pastime.
    True or False

11. For centuries shamans had fought in the spiritual realm with marauding shamans of illness, so, their art suggests, did they battle in the spiritual realm with the colonists.
    True or False

12. Bushman rock art itself and the belief system in which it was embedded is much more complex than was ever thought.
    True or False

13. As another organizing factor in music, whether regular or irregular, tonality may be more important than rhythm.
    True or False

14. The music of a marginalized group of former slaves eventually captivated the entire world, helping their descendants to escape their marginal status.
    True or False

15. In the United States, the arts often are seen as something of a frill, something to be engaged in for personal enjoyment apart from more productive pursuits or to provide pleasure for others, or both.
    True or False

16. A true myth is basically religious in that it provides a rationale for religious beliefs and practices.
    True or False

17. For the most part, legends and myths are the products solely of nonliterate, non-industralized societies.
    True or False

18. An art form that has developed recently is tattooing. It involves the puncturing and coloring of human skin with symbolic designs.
    True or False

19. Almost anything humans can lay their hands on can become an object of artistic expression-skin, hair, dress, dwellings, vehicles, weapons, utensils, etc.
   True or False

20. Some form of visual art is a part of every historically known human culture.
   True or False

21. Music is of little importance in the cultural preservation and revitalization efforts of indigenous peoples.
   True or False

Short Answer

1. As a type of symbolic expression, visual art may be representational or abstract. Discuss these two categories of visual art.

2. Describe the functional purposes of tattooing.

3. Explain the process by which tattooing has expanded in the U.S. from a working-class folk art into a more widespread and often refined aesthetic practice.

4. What meaning do tattoos have for middle-class North Americans?

Practice Essays

1. Many famous biographies or novels about artists in the West stress the individual creativity of the artist (for example, James Joyce's *Portrait of the Artist as a Young Man*). Artists are portrayed as people who have the vision to rise above and beyond the social and cultural conditions into which they were born, sometimes even crossing the boundaries of normality as typically defined by society. How is this vision of the artist different from the conception of artists held by non-Western societies?

2. Discuss art's general meaning. What is art's role in Bushman communities?

3. Bushman rock art extends beyond the generation of religious experience to the negotiation of political power. Demonstrate why this is so.

4. Discuss why it is important to protect the cultural heritages of tribal peoples. Why is it of concern to anthropologists?

5. Discuss the influence the African American experience has had on American music.

6. What are the social functions of music? Provide examples.

7. Art in all its forms has countless functions beyond providing aesthetic pleasure. Discuss some of the functions of art.

8. Art can and does play a role in indigenous rights efforts. Explain art's role i indigenous people's efforts to gain their rights.

Solutions

Fill-in-the-Blank

1. folklore
2. popular
3. Abenaki
4. psuedo-historical
5. West Africa
6. Bedouins
7. ethnomusicolgy
8. tonality
9. pentatonic system
10. polyrythm
11. America's Northwest coast
12. basketry
13. entopic phenomena

Multiple-Choice Practice Questions

1. E
2. E
3. D
4. C
5. D
6. E
7. C
8. C
9. A
10. E
11. A
12. A
13. C
14. B
15. C
16. A
17. D
18. E
19. C
20. E
21. E
22. D
23. C
24. C
25. D
26. E
27. B
28. E
29. D
30. C

True/False Practice Questions

1. T
2. T
3. T
4. T
5. F
6. F
7. F
8. T
9. F
10. F
11. T
12. T
13. F
14. F
15. T
16. T
17. F
18. F
19. T
20. T
21. F

Chapter 15

Processes of Change

Synopsis

Chapter 15 discusses the mechanisms of cultural change and examines anthropology's role in the changes sweeping the world. The use of the term "modernization" is considered from a cross-cultural perspective.

What You Should Learn from This Chapter

I. Understand how cultures change and the mechanisms involved:
    A. innovation
    B. diffusion
    C. cultural loss
    D. acculturation

II. Understand why the field of applied anthropology developed.

III. Understand how societies react to forcible change:
    A. syncretism
    B. revitalization movements

IV. Understand the process of modernization and its effect on societies.

Key Terms and Names

acculturation
applied anthropology
diffusion
Eric R. Wolf
Franz Boas
genocide
integrative mechanism
modernization

primary innovation
progress
rebellion
revolution
secondary innovation
structural differentiation
syncretism
tradition

Exercise

Briefly identify and locate the following cultures.

1. Skolt Lapps

2. Shuar

3. Ju/'hoansi

4. Wauja

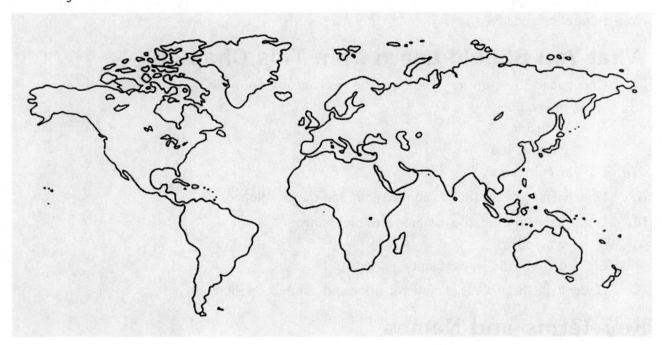

Exercise

Review Questions

1. Distinguish between primary and secondary innovation.

2. Provide an example of primary innovation.

3. Why is it that cultural context provides the means for innovation to occur?

4. What things have European Americans borrowed from American Indians?

5. What is meant by cultural loss?

6. Describe the nature of acculturation.

7. What three factors seem to be underlying causes of genocide?

8. What does the field of applied anthropology attempt to accomplish?

9. How did the Trobriand Islanders react to the British game of cricket?

10. What is the purpose of revitalization movements?

11. What are the precipitators of rebellion and revolution?

12. What is the problem with the term "modernization"?

13. What are the four sub-processes of modernization?

14. What is meant by the "culture of discontent"?

Fill-in-the-Blank

1. Innovations based on the chance discovery of some new principle are called _____ innovations, while innovations resulting from the deliberate application of these principles are called _____ innovations.

2. The spread of customs or practices from one culture to another is called _____ .

3. According to Ralph Linton, as much as _____ percent of a culture's content is due to borrowing.

4. _____ occurs when groups with different cultures come into intensive, firsthand contact and one or both groups experience massive cultural changes.

5. One society may retain its culture but lose its autonomy, becoming a _____ , _____ , or _____ within the dominant culture.

6. The extermination of one people by another is called _____ .

7. The field of _____ anthropology uses anthropological knowledge and techniques for practical purposes.

8. The applied work of anthropologist _____ helped reform the U.S. government's immigration policies.

9. Under conditions of acculturation, indigenous populations may blend foreign traits with those of their own culture to form a new cultural system. This response is called _____ .

10. The Trobrianders blended indigenous traditions with the British game of _____ .

11. _____ movements are deliberate attempts by members of a society to construct a more satisfactory culture.

12. A revitalization movement that attempts to bring back a destroyed but not forgotten way of life is called a _____ or revivalistic movement.

13. A revitalization movement that attempts to resurrect a suppressed, outcast group that has its own special subcultural ideology and has occupied an inferior social position for a long time is called _____ .

14. Revolutions have occurred only during the last _____ years, since the emergence of centralized systems of political authority.

15. Modernization refers to the process of cultural and socioeconomic change whereby developing societies become more similar to _____ industrialized societies.

16. The _____ aspect of modernization means a shift in population from rural areas to cities.

17. The Skolt Lapps in the country of _____ traditionally supported themselves by fishing and reindeer herding.

18. The Shuar Indians promoted cooperative _____ ranching as their new economic base.

19. By the early 1970s the United States, encompassing 6 percent of the world's population, was consuming about _____ percent of the world's output of copper, coal, and oil.

Multiple-Choice Practice Questions

1. In New England, the culture of English speakers replaced the various cultures of Native Americans living along the coast. Your text says that this occurred because _____.
   a. English-speaking culture was superior to Native American culture
   b. Native American culture was superior to English-speaking culture
   c. it is inevitable that English speakers will replace other cultures that they encounter
   d. a combination of accidental factors contributed to the success of English speakers in establishing colonies along coastal New England
   e. the success of English speakers was only a temporary setback for the progressive development of Native American culture

2. The chance discovery of some new principle that can be applied in a variety of ways is called _____.

    a. primary innovation

    b. primary syncretism

    c. applied anthropology

    d. millenarism

    e. diffusion

3. The deliberate use of basic ideas in some practical application, such as making use of the knowledge of how electricity works to develop the telephone, is called _____.

    a. revitalization

    b. millenarism

    c. modernization

    d. integrative mechanism

    e. secondary innovation

4. Copernicus's discovery that the earth orbits the sun rather than vice versa _____.

    a. was a primary innovation that met the cultural goals and needs of his time

    b. was a primary innovation that was out of step with the needs, values, and goals of the time

    c. was a secondary innovation that put into application the discovery by Ptolemy that heavenly bodies moved on crystalline spheres around the earth

    d. was a secondary innovation that was deliberately developed by Copernicus to destroy the Polish Church

    e. resulted from diffusion of ideas from India

5. According to the North American anthropologist Ralph Linton, about 90 percent of any culture's content comes from _____.

    a. primary innovation

    b. diffusion

    c. invention

    d. syncretism

    e. revolution

6. In biblical times, chariots and carts were widespread in the Middle East, but by the sixth century the roads had deteriorated so much that wheeled vehicles were replaced by camels. This illustrates that cultural change is sometimes due to _____.

    a. primary invention

    b. secondary invention

    c. diffusion

    d. revitalization

    e. cultural loss

7. As a result of prolonged firsthand contact between societies A and B, which of the following might happen?
    a. Society A might wipe out society B, with it becoming a new dominant society
    b. Society A might retain its distinctive culture but lose its autonomy and come to survive as a subculture such as a caste or ethnic group
    c. Society A might be wiped out by society B, with only a few scattered refugees living as members of the dominant society
    d. The cultures of A and B might fuse, becoming a single culture with elements of both
    e. "Society A might retain its distinctive culture but lose its autonomy and come to survive as a subculture such as a caste or ethnic group", "Society A might be wiped out by society B, with only a few scattered refugees living as members of the dominant society" and "The cultures of A and B might fuse, becoming a single culture with elements of both"

8. The extermination of one group of people by another, often deliberately and in the name of progress, is called _____.
    a. genocide
    b. acculturation
    c. diffusion
    d. applied anthropology
    e. primary innovation

9. The field of applied anthropology developed _____.
    a. through efforts to help the poor in North American society
    b. in sociology classrooms
    c. in industry
    d. in colonial situations
    e. through the efforts of women opposed to prohibition

10. In acculturation, subordinate groups will often incorporate new cultural elements into their own culture, creating a blend of old and new; a reinterpretation of new cultural elements to fit them with already existing traditions is called _____.
    a. syncretism
    b. innovation
    c. diffusion
    d. integrative mechanism
    e. modernization

11. A deliberate attempt by members of society to construct a more satisfying culture may be called _____.
    a. a secondary innovation
    b. a revitalization movement
    c. an enervating movement
    d. syncretism
    e. a primary innovation

12. Which of the following is/are considered to be important precipitators of rebellion and revolution?
    a. A sudden reversal of recent economic advances
    b. The media no longer support the government
    c. The established leadership loses prestige
    d. A strong, charismatic leader organizes attacks on the existing government
    e. "A sudden reversal of recent economic advances", "The media no longer support the government", "The established leadership loses prestige" and "A strong, charismatic leader organizes attacks on the existing government"

13. The term "modernization" _____.
    a. is a relativistic rather than ethnocentric concept
    b. refers to the process of cultural and socioeconomic change whereby societies acquire the characteristics of industrialized societies
    c. refers to a global and all-encompassing process whereby modern cities gradually deteriorate
    d. can be used to show that all societies go through the same stages of evolutionary development, culminating in the urban-industrial state
    e. is not used by anthropologists

14. As modernization occurs, which of the following changes are likely to follow?
    a. Literacy increases
    b. Religion decreases
    c. Kinship plays a less significant role
    d. Social mobility increases
    e. Literacy increases, Religion decreases, Kinship plays a less significant role and Social mobility increases

15. The division of a single role (which serves several functions) into two or more roles (each with a single specialized function) is called _____.
    a. millenarization
    b. modernization
    c. structural differentiation
    d. industrialization
    e. diffusion

16. Changes in Skolt Lapp society occurred because _____.
    a. men switched from reindeer herding to other sources of income
    b. the number of reindeer declined
    c. snowmobiles were used to herd reindeer
    d. society became hierarchical
    e. women became more powerful than men

17. The indigenous people whom Pedro Alvares Cabral encountered in his "discovery" of Brazil in 1500.

    a. Yanomami

    b. Shuar

    c. Mekranoti

    d. Pataxo

    e. Inca

18. The Brazilian Indian service.

    a. BIA

    b. FOIRN

    c. NGOs

    d. FUNAI

    e. CIMI

19. _____ are street beggars that wander the streets in all major cities of Brazil.

    a. Fandango

    b. Pobres

    c. Mendingo

    d. Gente de las calles

    e. Gente sin casas

20. The most common pattern characterizing violence against indigenous people in Brazil is _____.

    a. racism

    b. impunity (guilty party gets away with crime)

    c. massacres

    d. illegal detention

    e. police brutality

21. When people are able to keep faith with their traditions in the face of powerful outside domination, the result is _____.

    a. depression

    b. assimilation

    c. cretinism

    d. gratification

    e. syncretism

22. Over his career of 35 years of scholarly and applied work, _____, has made pioneering contributions to the development of applied anthropology and to anthropology's role in public policy and service.

    a. R.J. Gordon

    b. Michael M. Horowitz

    c. Pierre Van Den Berghe

    d. George Augustus Robinson

    e. August Dvorak

23. Horowitz's tireless dedication has been critical in institutionalizing anthropology as an applied science in international development organizations like which of the following?

    a. Nasdaq

    b. the World Bank

    c. USAID

    d. the Food and Agriculture Organization (FAO)

    e. the World Bank, USAID and the Food and Agriculture Organization (FAO)

24. The ultimate source of all change is _____.

    a. religion

    b. war

    c. innovation

    d. the weather

    e. biological

25. _____ occurs when two cultures lose their separate identities and form a single culture, as expressed by the "melting pot" ideology of Anglo-American culture in the United States.

    a. Extinction

    b. Corruption

    c. Dissolution

    d. Synthesis

    e. Merger

26. In 1637 a deliberate attempt was made to destroy the Pequot Indians by setting fire to their village at Mystic, Connecticut and then shooting down all those who sought to escape being burned alive. This is considered an act of _____.

    a. attrition

    b. contrition

    c. absolution

    d. genocide

    e. fratricide

27. In the present century, the scope of applied anthropology has broadened. Early on, the applied work of _____, considered by some to be the father of American anthropology, was instrumental in reforming U.S. immigration policies.
    a. Robert Lowie
    b. Napoleon Chagnon
    c. Walter Goldschmidt
    d. E. Adamson Hoebel
    e. Franz Boas

28. _____ movements that attempt to revive traditional ways of the past are not restricted to "underdeveloped" countries; in the U.S., the Reverend Pat Robertson is a leader in such a movement.
    a. New Age
    b. Mystical
    c. Revitalization
    d. Nostalgic
    e. Revolutionary

29. The process of modernization can be best understood as consisting of several subprocesses. Which of the following are subprocesses of modernization?
    a. extraterrestrial development
    b. technological development
    c. agricultural development
    d. weapons development
    e. technological development and agricultural development

30. Whereas most items for daily use were once made at home, such as butter, almost everything we use today is the product of specialized production, as is the butter we buy in the supermarket. This is a case of _____.
    a. urbanization
    b. industrialization
    c. structural differentiation
    d. productive progress
    e. efficient productivity

31. The gap between the rich and poor people of the world is widening rather than narrowing. This has led to the development of what anthropologist Paul Magnarella has called a new _____.
    a. "culture of poverty."
    b. "culture of unrealized dreams."
    c. "culture of unrealistic expectations."
    d. "culture of discontent."
    e. "class of have nots."

32. _____ is the massive change that comes about with the sort of intensive, firsthand contact that occurs when dominant societies forcefully expand their activities beyond their borders, leading less powerful societies to abandon their traditional cultures in favor of the foreign.
    a. Assimilation
    b. Integration
    c. Acculturation
    d. Adaptation
    e. Accomodation

33. The English crossed the Atlantic Ocean equipped with the political and military techniques for dominating other peoples; in addition they came with the ideology of _____, which they believed justified the dispossessing of America's indigenous peoples.
    a. democracy
    b. socialism
    c. communism
    d. a just war
    e. Christianity

34. It was not until some time between _____ and _____ years ago that people recognized a highly practical application of fired clay and began using it to make pottery containers and cooking vessels.
    a. 9000 and 8500
    b. 15,000 and 10,000
    c. 30,000 and 25,000
    d. 7500 and 6000
    e. 3000 and 2500

35. The worldwide process of accelerated modernization in which all parts of the earth are becoming interconnected in one vast interrelated and all-encompassing system is known as

    _____.
    a. revolution.
    b. rebellion.
    c. acculturation.
    d. globalization.
    e. capitalism.

36. One of the first and most prominent anthropologists to focus on worldwide transformations was

    _____.
    a. Franz Boas.
    b. Eric Wolf.
    c. Laura Nader.
    d. Ralph Nader.
    e. John Swetnam.

Overcoming two of its deepest internal
    conflicts: racism and the lack of punishment for those guilty of crimes against indigenous
    people (impunity).
    True or False

5. Brazil's indigenous peoples have shown that they are not merely "remnants" of a once great
    past, but are fully capable of forging viable models for their future.
    True or False

6. The impact of Michael M. Horowitz's applied anthropological research has been by all
    standards minimal.
    True or False

7. Acts of genocide are a fairly recent phenomena.
    True or False

8. Each revitalization movement that has occurred in the United States has been unique and
    different from the other.
    True or False

9. By their very nature, all revolts are revolutionary in their consequences.
    True or False

10. Haviland has made it quite clear that genocide is always a deliberate act.
    True or False

11. Because stability is a striking feature of many cultures like the food foragers, subsistence
    farmers, and pastoralists these cultures are changeless.
    True or False

12. Frequently, rather than just adding new things to those already in existence, the acceptance of a
    new innovation leads to the loss of an older one.
    True or False

13. Genocide is not always a deliberate act.
    True or False

14. Progress, like adaptation, is a consequence rather than a cause of change.
    True or False

238

15. Wheeled vehicles virtually disappeared from Morocco to Afghanistan about 1500 years ago. They were replaced by camels because of a reversion to the past by the region's inhabitants.
True or False

16. The practical application of anthropology is thriving today as never before.
True or False

Practice Matching

Match the culture with its characteristic.

1. _____ Skolt Lapps
2. _____ Shuar
3. _____ Wauja
4. _____ Iranians
5. _____ Tasmanians

a. Established an Islamic government after a successful religious revitalization.
b. An Amazonian people who mobilized to protect their native lands.
c. Native Americans of Ecuador who formed a federation to protect their interests.
d. Arctic Scandinavians whose society was radically changed by the introduction of snowmobiles.
e. Indigenous people off the coast of Australia who were wiped out by Europeans.

Short Answer

1. What is action anthropology?

2. Explain why the Taliban movement in Afghanistan was considered a revitalization movement.

3. Why has it been suggested that it would be impossible for most peoples of the world to achieve something resembling a middle-class standard of living comparable to that of many people in the Western world in the near future?

Practice Essays

1. Describe the impact of modernization on Skolt Lapps, Shuar Indians, and Wauja.

2. In what ways can the rising tide of Islamic fundamentalism in the Middle East and other areas of the world be seen as a revitalization movement? Are there other terms from the chapter that could apply to this phenomenon? What might anthropology contribute to our understanding of such movements?

3. The violence that occurred on Indian Day in Brazil 1997 brought to the surface old problems and wounds that have never healed. Identify and discuss these old problems and wounds that still exist in Brazilian society.

4. Statistics gathered by the Indigenous Missionary Council show that not only is there an increase in violence against Brazil's indigenous people, but also in the kinds of aggression committed against them. Identify the new forms of aggression against the indigenous peoples of Brazil. How are these cases represented and reported in the national press and how are they dealt with by authorities? Are there patterns in the violence that characterize Indian/white relations?

5. Explain why revolution is a relatively recent phenomenon.

6. Discuss the contributions of Michael M. Horowitz to the development of applied anthropology and to anthropology's role in public policy and service.

7. Reactions of indigenous peoples to changes forced upon them vary considerably. Describe how various groups have reacted to forced change.

8. Belief in "progress" and its inevitability has important implications for North Americans as well as others. What are the implication? Explain.

9. Explain the difference between a rebellion and a revolution. Provide recent examples of both.

Solutions

Fill-in-the-Blank

1. primary, secondary
2. diffusion
3. 90
4. Acculturation
5. ethnic group, class, caste
6. genocide
7. applied
8. Franz Boas
9. syncretism
10. cricket
11. Revitalization
12. revolutionary
13. revolutionary
14. 200
15. Western
16. urbanization
17. Finland
18. cattle
19. 50

Multiple-Choice Practice Questions

1. D
2. A
3. E
4. B
5. B
6. E
7. E
8. A
9. D
10. A
11. B
12. E
13. B
14. E
15. C
16. C
17. D
18. D
19. C
20. B
21. E
22. B
23. E
24. C
25. E
26. D
27. E
28. C
29. E
30. C
31. D
32. C
33. D
34. A
35. D
36. B

True/False Practice

1. T
2. T
3. F
4. F
5. T
6. F
7. F
8. F
9. F
10. F
11. F
12. T
13. T
14. T
15. F
16. T

Practice Matching

1. D
2. C
3. B
4. A
5. E

Chapter 16

Global Challenges, Local Responses, and the Role of Anthropology

Synopsis

In this concluding chapter the text considers the role of anthropological knowledge in facing the world of the future.

What You Should Learn from This Chapter

I.   Understand the contribution anthropology can make in planning for humanity's future.

II.   Understand what a one-world culture is and the feasibility of such a system.

III.   Consider the problems facing humankind and some possible avenues of solution.

Key Terms

Cultural pluralism
Culture of discontent
Ethnic resurgence
Global culture
Pluralistic society
Multiculturalism

Structural power
Hard power
Soft power
replacement reproduction
structural violence

Exercise

Review Questions

1.   What shortcomings are evident in future-oriented literature?

2.   What makes anthropologists uniquely suited to contribute to planning for the future?

3.   Can the globe today be described as a "one-world culture"?

4.   Why are predictions of a politically integrated world probably incorrect?

5.   Give an example of how misunderstandings might actually increase in a one-world culture.

6.   Give some contemporary examples of ethnic resurgence.

7. How does the concept of ethnocentrism interfere with cultural pluralism?

8. Provide examples of structural violence.

9. What is thought to be the immediate cause of world hunger? Provide examples.

10. Why is the suggestion that countries adopt agricultural practices similar to the United States not necessarily sound advice?

11. What is meant by the "exploitative world view"?

Fill-in-the-Blank

1. Anthropologists try to be _____ , meaning they take into account many interacting factors to understand the functioning of the complex whole.

2. Anthropologists have a _____ , meaning they take a long-term view of things.

3. Over the past five thousand years, political units have grown steadily _____ in size and _____ in number.

4. All large states have a tendency to _____ .

5. There are about _____ recognized states in the world today, but an estimated 5,000 national groups.

6. An important force for global unity are the _____ corporations that cut across national boundaries.

7. The separation of whites and blacks in South Africa under the domination of the white minority was a system called _____ .

8. About _____ of the population of the world is nonwhite.

9. A great deal of the violence in the world is not due to the unique and personal decisions of individuals but to social, political, and economic conditions; this is referred to as _____ violence.

10. The population of the world today is about _____ .

11. The cause of world hunger is not so much the ability to produce food but the ability to _____ it effectively.

12. _____ rain, caused in part by smokestack gases, is causing damage to lakes, forests, and ground water.

13. All civilizations have an _____ world view that tends to promote ecologically unsound cultural practices.

14. Replacement reproduction refers to a rate of reproduction in which a couple have no more than _____ children.

Multiple-Choice Practice Questions

1. Most people plan for the future by looking at trends in _____.
    a. ancient history
    b. hemlines
    c. third-world countries
    d. food supplies
    e. recent history

2. Anthropologists are trained to develop effective predictions of the future because they are _____.
    a. aware of cultural relativity
    b. good at seeing how parts fit together into a large whole
    c. trained to have an evolutionary perspective
    d. able to see short-term trends in long-term perspective
    e. "aware of cultural relativity", "good at seeing how parts fit together into a large whole", "trained to have an evolutionary perspective" and "able to see short-term trends in long-term perspective"

3. Over the past five thousand years, political units have _____.
    a. grown steadily smaller in size
    b. grown steadily larger in size and fewer in number
    c. eliminated multinational corporations
    d. promoted individual freedoms
    e. eliminated slavery

4. Multinational corporations _____.
    a. have been widespread in Western culture since medieval times
    b. were very common during the colonial period
    c. have become a major force in the world today since the 1950s
    d. have been disintegrating since the 1950s
    e. promote relativistic rather than ethnocentric ideas

5. Which of the following expresses the **negative** consequences of multinational corporations on the international and domestic scenes?
    a. Multinational corporations cross-cut nations and thus achieve a global unity
    b. Multinational corporations have become a major force in the world since the 1950s
    c. Multinational corporations have become so powerful that they have been able to influence government decisions so that they benefit the company rather than the people
    d. Multinational corporations are products of the technological revolution
    e. They have developed sophisticated data-processing techniques that enable them to keep track of worldwide operations

6. Cultural pluralism _____.
   a. may constitute a temporary stage in a process of integration into a single melting-pot culture
   b. implies the absence of bigotry and racism
   c. implies respect for the cultural traditions of other peoples
   d. may result from conquest or from several culturally distinct groups occupying an area that eventually becomes unified as a larger political entity
   e. "may constitute a temporary stage in a process of integration into a single melting-pot culture", "implies the absence of bigotry and racism", "implies respect for the cultural traditions of other peoples" and "may result from conquest or from several culturally distinct groups occupying an area that eventually becomes unified as a larger political entity"

7. Which of the following represent the **negative** consequences of ethnocentrism?
   a. By believing that another culture is inferior to yours, you can, with a sense of righteousness, destroy its temples, cottage industry, polygynous practices, and so on in order to bring it into line with your culture's standards of appropriate behavior and belief
   b. Ethnocentrism confers a sense of pride in and loyalty to one's own cultural traditions
   c. Ethnocentrism provides a feeling of psychological gratification that one is living the right kind of life
   d. Ethnocentrism contributes to a sense of personal worth
   e. Ethnocentrism strengthens social solidarity

8. _____ is violence produced by social, political, and economic structures rather than by the unique and personal decisions of individuals.
   a. Torture
   b. Modernization
   c. Structural violence
   d. Insanity
   e. Religion

9. The change from subsistence farming to cash crops _____.
   a. enables farmers to enlarge their holdings and feed their families more effectively
   b. results in the relocation of subsistence farmers to urban areas or to lands ecologically unfit for farming
   c. leads to the decline of multinational corporations
   d. supports cultural pluralism
   e. leads to revitalization

10. The main reason an Asian wet-rice farmer might choose not to adopt North American techniques of intensive agriculture is because _____.

    a.   he or she cannot afford to buy the chemical products typically used in this type of agriculture

    b.   the North American method requires at least eight calories of energy to be expended for every calorie produced, whereas the wet-rice farmer produces three hundred calories for every calorie he or she invests

    c.   the North American method produces toxic substances that destroy delicate ecological balances

    d.   he or she predicts that the North American method, while successful for a short period of time, is sowing the seeds of its own destruction

    e.   "he or she cannot afford to buy the chemical products typically used in this type of agriculture", "the North American method requires at least eight calories of energy to be expended for every calorie produced, whereas the wet-rice farmer produces three hundred calories for every calorie he or she invests", "the North American method produces toxic substances that destroy delicate ecological balances" and "he or she predicts that the North American method, while successful for a short period of time, is sowing the seeds of its own destruction"

11. Pollution, although a worldwide consequence of certain agricultural and industrial activities, is more of a problem in _____ because chemicals that may be banned in richer nations can be used more easily.

    a.   poor countries

    b.   industrialized countries

    c.   arctic countries

    d.   Mediterranean countries

    e.   ocean areas

12. If a country achieves "replacement reproduction," this means that _____.

    a.   people produce only enough children to replace themselves when they die

    b.   each reproductive couple has no more children

    c.   its population will immediately stop growing

    d.   its population will continue to grow for another fifty years

    e.   every other generation can have children

13. The most extreme form of female genital mutilation.

    a.   female circumcision

    b.   breast implantation

    c.   infibulation

    d.   appendectomy

    e.   tonsillectomy

14. The most dramatic illustrations of the tendency for states to come apart recently would be which of the following?

    a. The breakup of the Soviet Union

    b. The breakup of Yugoslavia

    c. The separation of East Timor from Indonesia

    d. The separation of Vietnam into North and South Vietnam

    e. The breakup of the Soviet Union, The breakup of Yugoslavia and The separation of East Timor from Indonesia

15. The dramatic revival of pastoral nomadism in Mongolia would be an example of _____.

    a. cultural pluralism

    b. cultural decline

    c. nationalistic pride

    d. ethnic backwardness

    e. resistance to modernization

16. Presently in the world, the _____ richest individuals have a combined wealth equal to the annual income of the poorest 47 percent of the entire world's population.

    a. 125

    b. 225

    c. 350

    d. 472

    e. 555

17. The immediate cause of world hunger has more to do with which of the following?

    a. food production

    b. food distribution

    c. food storage

    d. warfare

    e. food distribution and warfare

18. The world's population is projected to peak in 49 years at about _____ billion people.

    a. 20

    b. 7.5

    c. 9.37

    d. 8.35

    e. 5.23

19. Which of the following would make the anthropologist well-equipped to make valid projections about the world's future?
    a.   their holistic perspective
    b.   their evolutionary perspective
    c.   their 100 years of cross-cultural research
    d.   their familiarity with alternative ways to deal with a wide variety of problems
    e.   "their holistic perspective", "their evolutionary perspective", "their 100 years of cross-cultural research" and "their familiarity with alternative ways to deal with a wide variety of problems"

20. Which of the following groups of women experience body mutilation as part of engendering rites?
    a.   North American
    b.   Sudanese
    c.   Filipino
    d.   Mexican
    e.   North American and Sudanese

21. After a 10-year intensive study of relations between producers and consumers of products and services, anthropologist _____ found repeated and documented offenses by business that cannot be handled by present complaint mechanisms, either in or out of court.
    a.   Margaret Mead
    b.   Laura Nader
    c.   Ruth Benedict
    d.   Linda Coco
    e.   Howard Zinn

22. Sometimes, resistance to modernization takes the form of a _____ reaction, as it did in Iran and as is happening today in Algeria.
    a.   revivalistic
    b.   rebellious
    c.   fundamentalist
    d.   pluralistic
    e.   allergic

23. The problem with _____ is that it all too easily can be taken as a charter for manipulating other cultures for the benefit of one's own, even though this does not have to be the choice.
    a.   ethnocentrism
    b.   ambivalence
    c.   provincialism
    d.   prejudice
    e.   narrow-mindedness

24. Which of the following are reasons impoverished people tend to have so many children?

    a. Children are their main resource

    b. Children provide a needed labor pool to work farms

    c. Children are the only source of security for the elderly

    d. Infant mortality rates are unusually high in impoverished areas

    e. "Children are their main resource", "Children provide a needed labor pool to work farms", "Children are the only source of security for the elderly" and "Infant mortality rates are unusually high in impoverished areas"

25. In order to solve the problems brought about by global structural violence it has been suggested that dramatic changes in cultural values and motivations, as well as social institutions, will be required. Which of the following would have to change to help solve the problems due to structural violence?

    a. the emphasis on individual self-interest

    b. uncontrolled materialism

    c. a sense of social responsibility

    d. excessive consumption

    e. "the emphasis on individual self-interest", "uncontrolled materialism" and "excessive consumption"

26. However humanity changes biologically, _____ remains the chief means by which humans try to solve their problems.

    a. technology

    b. religion

    c. faith in humankind

    d. military might

    e. culture

27. Since _____ seems unstoppable, we are compelled to ask: How can the thousands of different cultures, developed in the course of centuries if not millennia, deal successfully with the multiple challenges hurled at them?

    a. assimilation

    b. acculturation

    c. global warming

    d. globalization

    e. industrialization

28. This vast, mountainous country is inhabited by several major ethnic groups, including the Pashtun who live mainly in the south, and Tajik, Uzbek, Hazara, and Turkmen who live mainly in the north. The country being described is _____.
   a. Turkey.
   b. Iraq.
   c. Uzbekistan.
   d. Chechnya.
   e. Afghanistan.

29. The Karen people's separatist movement is taking place in Myammar, formerly known as _____.
   a. Turkey.
   b. Burma.
   c. Croatia.
   d. India.
   e. Indonesia.

30. Although, of late, there has been a tendency for political units to fragment into smaller ones, there are instances of reunification. Best known is the 1990 reunification of _____.
   a. Ireland.
   b. Germany.
   c. Czechoslovakia.
   d. Korea.
   e. Indonesia.

31. In 1992 a Maya woman named _____ won the prestigious Nobel Peace Prize for her tireless work on behalf of indigenous rights.
   a. Eva Balam-Ek
   b. Luisa Che
   c. Raquel Maria Casas
   d. Rigoberta Menchu
   e. Maria Elena Ujpan

32. In the United States today more than _____ million adults are overweight or even obese.
   a. 50
   b. 10
   c. 15
   d. 25
   e. 100

True/False Practice Questions

1. Multinational corporations have constituted a strong force for global unity.
   True or False

2. Structural violence refers to violence produced by social, political, and economic structures rather than by the unique and personal decisions of individuals.
    True or False

3. The change from subsistence farming to cash crops leads to economic improvements in countries that made the change.
    True or False

4. Modernization refers to a situation in which groups with different ways of acting and thinking can interact socially with mutual respect.
    True or False

5. The question of choice is central to the story of how medicine and business generate controlling processes in the shaping of women's bodies.
    True or False

6. Sudanese and other African women, North American women, and others experience body mutilation as part of engendering rites.
    True or False

7. The American Society of Plastic and Reconstructive Surgery operates like a commercial enterprise instead of a medical society. They saturate the media to sell women breast implants. The author of the original study, Linda Coco, refers to this idea as "patriarchal capitalism."
    True or False

8. Social surveys indicate that, to the extent that women internalize the social imperative that they can enhance their lives by enhancing their breasts, they feel they are making the decision on their own.
    True or False

9. In the Sudan, the young girl is told that circumcision and infibulation are done to her not for her.
    True or False

10. According to Linda Coco, the operation on the female breast in North America does **not** hold the same symbolism and expression of cultural mandate as does infibulation in Sudan.
    True or False

11. The interest of Cultural Survival, Inc. is to preserve indigenous cultures in their original pristine condition so that they will be there to study and to serve as living museum exhibits.
    True or False

12. Much remains to be done to secure the survival of indigenous peoples in all parts of the world.
    True or False

13. The Native American attempts to secure greater political sovereignty are an indication that the United States is not immune to breakup.
    True or False

14. In Guatemala robberies, assaults, torture, and death threats against human rights groups, journalists, and nongovernmental organizations were on the increase in the year 2000.
    True or False

15. According to Haviland's textbook, most of the world's weapons of mass destruction are owned by whites.
True or False

16. The immediate cause of world hunger has less to do with warfare than with food production and food distribution.
True or False

17. Multinationals are an extremely new phenomena on the global scene, appearing first around the 1950s.
True or False

18. According to the original study "Standardizing the Body," the question of choice is central to the story of how medicine and business generate controlling processes in the shaping of women's bodies.
True or False

19. In so-called "underdeveloped" countries, women have become a source of cheap labor for large corporations, as subsistence farming has given way to mechanized farming.
True or False

20. It seems the more divergent cultural traditions are, the easier it is to make pluralism work.
True or False

21. Though a minority of the world's population, people in the developed countries consume the most resources and generate the bulk of hazardous wastes.
True or False

22. The United States, because of its Constitution and Bill of Rights, is immune to the kinds of separatist movements occurring in other countries around the globe.
True or False

23. The more divergent cultural traditions are, the more difficult it seems to make pluralism work.
True or False

24. Today, the top 100 companies control 33 percent of the world's assets, but employ only one percent of the world's workforce.
True or False

25. Today there are more underfed people in the world than overfed people.
True or False

26. Not all people who are overweight or obese are so because they eat too much junk food and have too little exercise.
True or False

Short Answer Head

1. In 1991 the Soviet Union broke-up into numerous independent republics. Identify those newly minted independent states.

2. The tendency for multi-ethnic states to splinter can be seen in separatist movements that arise. Identify the separatist movements that have arisen recently in various countries.

3. What is multiculturalism?

4. Why can it be said that global corporations are products of the technology revolution?

5. Define structural power.

6. Some dramatic changes in cultural values and motivations, as well as in social institutions, are required if humans are going to realize a sustainable future for generations to come. What changes in cultural values and motivations need to occur?

Practice Essays

1. The effort to reduce population growth faces enormous cultural obstacles. Illustrate this by describing Chinese efforts to promote one-child families, and consider whether Western planners should attempt to encourage similar efforts in the Islamic world, where birth control is prohibited on religious grounds. Where does appropriate global planning run up against the charge of ethnocentrism or cultural imperialism?

2. One of the most heated debates arising from the public health concern over breast implants is whether the recipient's decision is voluntary or whether control is disguised as free will. Explain what is meant by this.

3. What is the main interest of the advocacy group Cultural Survival, Inc.? Describe what they are trying to do for indigenous peoples. What are some of their success stories?

4. Despite a worldwide trend toward "Westernization," and despite the pressure for traditional cultures to disappear, it is clear that cultural differences are still very much with us in the world today. In fact, a tendency for peoples globally to resist modernization, and in some cases retreat from it, is strengthening. How can this be? Explain, using examples.

5. Discuss the rise of multinational corporations and their impact on the domestic as well as the international scene.

6. Debate the pros and cons of a "globalization."

7. Identify and discuss the problems of structural violence.

8. Solving the problems of the global society depends on, among other things, lessening the gap between the living standards of the impoverished and developed countries. How can this be accomplished?

9. Explain how global corporations might be a force for worldwide political integration.

10. In their never-ending search for cheap labor, multinational corporations have returned to a practice once seen in the textile mills of 19th century New England. Identify and discuss this practice.

11. There are two major interacting forces in the worldwide arena "hard power" and "soft power." Define these two types of power and discuss how they interact. Provide examples.

12. A key factor in the world's food crisis is a dramatic rise in the world's population. Discuss population growth worldwide.

13. There are actually two "cultures of discontent." One exists in poor countries and the other is emerging in wealthy countries. Discuss each of the "cultures of discontent" and describe how they came about.

Solutions

Fill-in-the-Blank

1. holistic
2. historical perspective
3. larger, fewer
4. come apart
5. 190
6. multinational
7. apartheid
8. two-thirds
9. structural
10. 6-7 billion
11. distribute
12. Acid
13. materialistic
14. two

Multiple-Choice Practice Questions

1. E
2. E
3. B
4. C
5. C
6. E
7. A
8. C
9. B
10. A
11. A
12. A
13. C
14. E
15. E
16. B
17. E
18. C
19. E
20. E
21. B
22. C
23. A
24. E
25. E
26. E
27. D
28. E
29. B
30. B
31. D
32. A

True/False Practice Questions

1. T
2. T
3. F
4. F
5. T
6. T
7. T
8. T
9. F
10. F
11. F
12. T
13. T
14. T
15. T
16. F
17. F
18. T
19. T
20. F
21. T
22. F
23. T
24. T
25. F
26. T